Black American Literature
Poetry

Edited by

Darwin T. Turner

University of Michigan

65400

Charles E. Merrill Publishing Company
A Bell & Howell Company
Columbus, Ohio

CHARLES E. MERRILL LITERARY TEXTS

Under the General Editorship of
Matthew J. Bruccoli and Joseph Katz

Anthologies by genre, period, theme, or other significant principle for the study of American Literature. Each volume provides reliable texts introduced by a noted authority.

Textual Note

This volume presents authoritative texts for all material. The selections are reprinted from their original appearances as specified in each case.

Copyright © 1969 by Charles E. Merrill Publishing Company, Columbus, Ohio. All rights reserved. No part of this book may be reproduced in any form, electronic or mechanical, including photocopy, recording, or any information storage and retrieval system without permission in writing from the publisher.

ISBN: 0-675-09499-2

Library of Congress Catalog Card Number: 71-99194

3   4   5   6   7   8   9   10 — 76   75   74

Printed in the United States of America

To
my brother Charles
and
my aunt Mamie

Acknowledgments

Let me take this opportunity to express a very deep appreciation to Mrs. Fannie Garrison and Mrs. Nina Bridges, who helped type this work, and to Miss Myrtle Howard, whose general assistance was invaluable. I wish also to express gratitude to my wife, Jeanne, who endured while I wrote.

"On being brought from Africa to America," "To the University of Cambridge in New-England," and "Goliath of Gath" from *Poems on Various Subjects, Religious and Moral* by Phillis Wheatley (London: A. Bell, 1773).

"The Swan-Vain Pleasures," "The Powers of Love," "To a Departing Favorite," "The Eye of Love," and "The Setting Sun" from *The Poetical Works of George M. Horton, The Colored Bard of North Carolina* by George M. Horton (Hillsborough, North Carolina: D. Heartt, 1845).

"Frederick Douglass," "Ode to Ethiopia," "Ere Sleep Comes Down to Soothe the Weary Eyes," and "An Ante-Bellum Sermon," originally from *Lyrics of Lowly Life* by Paul Laurence Dunbar (New York: Dodd, Mead and Company, 1896). Reprinted by permission of Dodd, Mead & Company, Inc. from *The Complete Poems of Paul Laurence Dunbar*.

"When a Feller's Itchin' to be Spanked" from *Lyrics of Sunshine and Shadow* by Paul Laurence Dunbar (New York: Dodd, Mead and Company, 1905).

"Rhapsody," "Hymn for the Slain in Battle," "To ———," "If I Could Touch," and "Two Questions" from *Lyrics of Life and Love* by W. S. Braithwaite (Boston: Herbert B. Turner, 1904).

"Sence You Went Away" from *Fifty Years and Other Poems* (Boston: Cornhill, 1917), by permission of The Viking Press, Inc. Copyright © 1917 by James Weldon Johnson. All rights reserved.

"The Creation" from *God's Trombones* by James Weldon Johnson (New York: Viking, 1927), by permission of The Viking Press, Inc. Copyright © 1927 by The Viking Press, Inc., renewed 1955 by Grace Nail Johnson.

"Black Woman," "Credo," "The Suppliant," and "To William Stanley Braithwaite" from *Bronze: A Book of Verse* by Georgia Douglas Johnson (Boston: B. J. Brimmer, 1922).

"Outcast," "Enslaved," "Africa," "America," "The Lynching," "If We Must Die," "Flame-Heart," "The Harlem Dancer," and "Flower of Love" from *Harlem Shadows* by Claude McKay (New York: Harcourt, Brace & Co., 1922). Copyright © 1922 by Harcourt, Brace & Company. Reprinted by permission of Twayne Publishers.

Last 119 lines from *The Blue Meridian* , "Five Vignettes," "The Lost Dancer," and "At Sea" published here for the first time by permission of Liveright Publishing Corporation. Copyright © 1969 by Marjorie C. Toomer.

"Heritage," "From the Dark Tower," "Song in Spite of Myself," "Magnets," and "For Paul Laurence Dunbar" from *On These I Stand* by Countee Cullen (New York: Harper & Brothers, 1947); "Heritage" and "For Paul Laurence Dunbar," copyright 1925 by Harper & Brothers, renewed 1953 by Ida M. Cullen; "From the Dark Tower," copyright 1927 by Harper & Brothers, renewed 1955 by Ida M. Cullen; "Magnets," copyright 1935 by Harper & Brothers, renewed 1963 by Ida M. Cullen. Reprinted by permission of Harper & Row, Publishers.

"Dream Variation," "Epilogue," and "The Weary Blues": Copyright © 1926 by Alfred A. Knopf, Inc. and renewed 1954 by Langston Hughes. Reprinted from *Selected Poems,* by Langston Hughes, by permission of the publisher. (The three texts used in this volume were taken from *The Weary Blues* by Langston Hughes.)

"Theme for English B" and "College Formal: Renaissance Casino" from *Montage of a Dream Deferred* by Langston Hughes. Reprinted by permission of Harold Ober Associates Incorporated. Copyright © 1951 by Langston Hughes.

"Madam and Her Madam," copyright 1948 by Alfred A. Knopf, Inc. Reprinted from *Selected Poems,* by Langston Hughes, by permission of the publisher. (The text used in this volume was taken from *One-Way Ticket* by Langston Hughes.)

"Southern Mansion," and "Nocturne at Bethesda" from *Personals* by Arna Bontemps (London: Paul Breman, 1963), by permission of Harold Ober Associates Incorporated. Copyright © 1963 by Arna Bontemps.

"Slim Greer," "Long Gone," "Return," and "Southern Road" from *Southern Road* by Sterling A. Brown (New York: Harcourt, Brace, 1932), by permission of the author. Copyright © 1932 by Harcourt, Brace and Company.

"Dark Symphony" from *Rendezvous with America* by Melvin B. Tolson (New York: Dodd, Mead, 1944), by permission of Dodd, Mead, & Company, Inc. Copyright © 1944 by Dodd, Mead, & Company, Inc."

"Runagate, Runagate" and "The Ballad of Nat Turner" from *Selected Poems* by Robert Hayden (New York: October House, 1966). Reprinted by permission of the October House, Inc. Copyright © 1966 by Robert Hayden.

"Sorrow Is the Only Faithful One," "For My Brother: VII," and "Open Letter" from *Powerful Long Ladder* by Owen Dodson. Copyright © 1946 by Farrar, Straus & Giroux, Inc. Reprinted by permission of Farrar, Strauss & Giroux, Inc.

"For My People" from *For My People* by Margaret Walker (New Haven: Yale University Press, 1942), by permission of Yale University Press. Copyright © 1942 by Yale University Press.

"Kitchenette Apartment," from *Selected Poems* (1963) by Gwendolyn Brooks, copyright 1945 by Gwendolyn Brooks Blakely; "The Woman-hood: I. 2," copyright 1949 by Gwendolyn Brooks Blakely. Reprinted by permission of Harper & Row, Publishers. (The texts used in this volume are the following: "Kitchenette Building" from *A Street in Bronzeville* by Gwendolyn Brooks, "The Womanhood: I. 2" from *The Bean Eaters* by Gwendolyn Brooks.) Reprinted by permission of Harper & Row, Publishers.

"The Womanhood: XV" is from *Annie Allen* by Gwendolyn Brooks, copyright 1949 by Gwendolyn Brooks Blakely. Reprinted by permission of Harper & Row, Publishers.

From *In the Mecca* (1968) by Gwendolyn Brooks: "Malcolm X," copyright © 1967 by Gwendolyn Brooks Blakely; "The Blackstone Rangers," copyright © 1968 by Gwendolyn Brooks Blakely. Reprinted by permission of Harper & Row, Publishers.

"Primitives" and "The Melting Pot" from *Cities Burning* by Dudley Randall. Copyright © 1968 by Dudley Randall. Reprinted by permission of the author and the publisher, Broadside Press.

"Nocturne" and "Alabama Centennial" from *Star by Star* by Naomi Long Madgett, copyright © 1965 by Naomi Long Madgett. Reprinted by permission of the author.

"The Sit-In," "Death," "Love," and "Sonnet Sequence: I and Finale" are from *Katharsis* by Darwin T. Turner, copyright © 1964 by Darwin T. Turner.

"Guest Lecturer" by Darwin T. Turner is published here for the first time. Copyright © 1969 by Darwin T. Turner.

"An Agony. As Now" and "The end of man is his beauty" from the *Dead Lecturer* by LeRoi Jones, copyright © 1964 by LeRoi Jones. Reprinted by permission of The Sterling Lord Agency.

"The Idea of Ancestry" and "He Sees Through Stone" from *Poems form Prison* by Etheridge Knight, copyright © 1968 by Etheridge Knight, Detroit, Michigan. Reprinted by permission of the publisher, Dudley Randall and Broadside Press, Detroit, Michigan.

"Education" and "Back Again, Home" from *Think Black* by Don L. Lee, copyright © by Don L. Lee. Reprinted by permission of the publisher, Dudley Randall and Broadside Press, Detroit, Michigan.

Contents

Introduction

A study of poetic creativity by Afro-Americans should begin not with compositions by individual writers but with the folk songs — the spirituals, the ballads, the work songs, and the secular songs. Folk songs do not depend upon the niceties of civilization — the formal education which lends literary models and the finances which permit the purchase of pen, ink, and paper. Folk singing requires only people who can voice their emotions rhythmically, melodiously, and imaginatively. Thus, it is the natural vehicle for poetic expression by people who are talented but illiterate and impoverished, as were the majority of black slaves and freedmen.

The songs deserve study. They reveal the artistic talent, the ideas, and the emotions of black Americans. Too often, consideration of this early art work has been restricted to those spirituals which obviously indicate the black man's reliance upon religion for comfort during his days of adversity. Other songs should be considered: those spirituals whose ambiguous phrasings may have signaled the slaves' intention to escape ("Steal Away"), those spirituals whose religious guise thinly veils their abolitionist content ("Go Down Moses" and "Oh, Mary, Don't You Weep"), those work songs which protest against drudgery and unjust abuse, and those ballads which create folk heroes like wicked Stackalee and proud John Henry.

Folk songs, however, reflect the art of an entire group. To examine the artistic talent of individuals one must concentrate on works which can be credited to individual authors. This present collection, therefore, is restricted to the work of representative black artists who have published volumes of poetry in the United States of America. Such a collection cannot pretend to demonstrate fully the artistic potential of a race: it does not include those unknown singers who never learned to write; it does not include those unknowns whose alien styles and thoughts dissuaded publishers from accepting their works. This collection does, however, offer a representative sampling of the kinds and quality of poetry written by black Americans.

It is not surprising that the first written poetry by black Americans issued from Northern and Eastern states, where slaves enjoyed greater freedom of educational opportunity than they experienced in the South. In 1746 Lucy Terry, a slave in Deerfield, Massachusetts, poetically described an Indian attack in "Bars Fight," the first poem known to have been composed by an African-American. Fourteen years later Jupiter Hammon, a slave on Long Island, published a poem entitled "An Evening Thought: Salvation by Christ, with Penitential Cries." And in 1773, Phillis Wheatley, a teenaged slave in Boston, published the first volume of black American poetry — *Poems on Various Subjects, Religious and Moral.*

Although Phillis Wheatley's poetry compares favorably with that which other Americans were writing at the time, these early poets in general are memorable only as historical curiosities, distinguished neither in style nor in thought. Undoubtedly, the conciliatory tone of Hammon's work and the non-racial attitude of much of Phillis Wheatley's poetry reflect the poets' awareness that their opportunities to learn and to publish depended upon the good will of their masters.

A slightly stronger cry for liberty sounded in the poetry of George Moses Horton who, in 1829, published *Hope of Liberty*, the first collection by a Southern slave. The title is appropriate for a work which Horton hoped would bring sufficient income to enable him to purchase his freedom. Nevertheless, most of the poems are not cries for liberty but sentimental songs like the love lyrics which he wrote on commission from students of the University of North Carolina at Chapel Hill. Like Hammon and Phillis Wheatley, Horton may have restrained himself from giving public offense to those upon whom his fortunes depended.

No such restriction troubled several free blacks who denounced slavery in their poetry during the generation preceding the Civil War. The most significant among this group were Frances E. W. Harper, James Whitfield, and James Madison Bell. The most popular was Frances Harper, abolitionist lecturer, temperance lecturer, and author of four books, the first — *Poems on Various Subjects* — published in 1854.

The first Afro-American to earn and maintain a national reputation as a poet, however, was Paul Laurence Dunbar, whom William Dean Howells described as the first American Negro to reveal innate artistic talent. One of the most popular American poets in the early years of the twentieth century, Dunbar became known chiefly for comic or sentimental dialect poems about slaves and freedmen — even though he also occasionally wrote poems of protest, and often wrote eloquent tributes to the Negro people and to individual Negroes. The reputation has persisted even though most of Dunbar's poetry was written in standard English. Dunbar was depressed that his "graceful lyrics," as he called them, were ignored while his "jingles in a broken tongue" were remembered; for he, like most black writers of his time, wished to demonstrate the cultural respectability of black Americans. They believed that America denied opportunity to black Americans only because, considering them slaves and savages, it failed to recognize their potential. Therefore, such men as Dunbar, Charles W. Chesnutt, and W. E. B. DuBois sought to prove, by reason and by example, that Afro-Americans were capable of moral responsibility, educated behavior, and cultural creativity in the approved traditions of America.

In Dunbar's poetry can be found the framework and the impulse for the three distinctive attitudes which Sterling Brown, Arthur Davis, and Ulysses Lee, in *The Negro Caravan* (1941), have identified among Afro-American poets during the first two decades of the twentieth century. One group of writers, including James E. Campbell and J. Mord Allen, continued the dialect tradition with its emphasis on rural life, sentimentality, and good humor. A second group used poetry as a vehicle for racial protest and defense. The most notable figures of this group were Joseph S. Cotter, Sr., Joseph S. Cotter, Jr., and Fenton Johnson. A third group echoed Dunbar's philosophy that the best poetry presents noble sentiments in beautiful language. W. S. Braithwaite, Leslie P. Hill, Georgia D. Johnson and others wrote lyrically about traditional subjects.

The third decade of the century featured the most exciting explosion of cultural activity which black Americans had ever experienced. Some observers found the character of the activity so distinctive that they described it as the "New Negro" movement. Others called it the "Negro Renaissance" or the "Harlem Renaissance." The term "Renaissance," however, may imply falsely that the culture of black Americans had died at some previous point. To the contrary, as must be evident from this brief history, black artists had not stopped working in the decade preceding the Twenties. But, during the Twenties, black artists were sought out, encouraged, supported, published, and honored by white Americans. In a sense then, black culture was not reborn but merely rediscovered or remembered.

Diverse merging forces produced this new era. After World War I, a wave of enthusiasm and idealism inspired black and white Americans. Afro-Americans had migrated North during the war; they had found jobs. Some black Americans had gone to England and to France, where they had found dignity and freedom. Some Americans looked enviously to the blacks as symbols of the joy, uninhibited emotion, and sexual freedom which young white Americans wanted, or thought they wanted. Others redirected towards their black countrymen the humanitarian sentiments which had been awakened by the war fought "to preserve democracy."

Black culture was the rage. Performers and non-performers crowded into dim clubs to hear the new sounds of jazz from "King" Oliver, Louis Armstrong, and Duke Ellington. White writers such as Eugene O'Neill, Sherwood Anderson, Carl van Vechten, Gertrude Stein, Dubose Heyward, and William Faulkner interpreted the Negro. Wealthy patrons supported black talent. Publishers accepted their works.

But, perhaps most important of all, such men as Alain Locke and Carl van Vechten brought black artists together. In America, black artists generally have been isolated. Social custom has restricted their relationships with their white contemporaries, and physical distance often has limited association with other black artists. Thus, separated from and often unfamiliar with the avant-garde ideas being discussed and practiced in their society, they have been forced to imitate the traditional style or to invent something novel. And, aware of the reluctance of white publishers to risk financial loss in experiments by black writers, they generally have clung to the traditional. From a historian's point of view, consequently, they often appear at the end of a literary tradition and rarely in the early stages of a new one. The mingling of black artists in Harlem during the Twenties, however, at least afforded them immediate awareness of the ideas circulating among artists of their own race. Significantly, the most avant-garde black poet of the Twenties was Jean Toomer, who gained access to the world of Hart Crane, Waldo Frank, Kenneth Burke, Gorham Munson, and *Dial* magazine.

Young poets responded to these forces with pride and confidence rarely evidenced by earlier Afro-Americans. They sought their individual identities in their racial heritage and their ancestral origins: Claude McKay wrote proudly of his Jamaican home; Countee Cullen boasted of the African impulses surging through his veins; Jean Toomer found his people in the red soil of Georgia. The poets explored their artistic heritage for new modes of expression: Langston Hughes experimented with ways to reproduce the soul and rhythm of jazz and the blues; James Weldon Johnson, an older poet, experimented with ways to reproduce the idiom, rhythm, and fervor of Negro sermons. Above all, they felt no shame in their color or their race. Countee Cullen and Waring Cuney described the rhythm and beauty of dark-skinned Americans. More significantly, some not only created characters resembling the comic stereotypes of white authors but even ridiculed their Negro protagonists with a freedom which comes only with self-assurance.

In reality, despite the proclamations that everything was new, the three dominant attitudes of the earlier decades shine through the transformations. Instead of imitating the tradition of satirical dialect poems about Southern Negroes, Langston Hughes wrote satirical poems about Northerners who spoke the dialect of Harlem. Claude McKay protested against racism as bitterly as any earlier writer had. And Countee Cullen and Arna Bontemps excelled the "graceful lyrics" of Dunbar and Braithwaite.

Therefore, one should not be blinded by the apparent aura of novelty in the poetry of the Harlem Renaissance. What is more important to recognize is the developing tendency towards realistic portraiture. Despite a number of idealized characterizations prompted by atavism, actual Afro-Americans are described in the poems of Countee Cullen and Langston Hughes.

The Harlem Renaissance was an era of poetic wealth in a decade of economic prosperity. For most of America, the Thirties were a decade of economic deprivation which, in poetry and other literary genres, inspired social protest, regionalism, and interest in workers and farmers. The new spirit is reflected in the work of Sterling Brown and Frank M. Davis, author of *Black Man's Verse* (1935) and *I Am the American Negro* (1937).

The late Thirties and early Forties were apprentice years for five major poets—Melvin B. Tolson, Robert Hayden, Margaret Walker, Owen Dodson, and Gwendolyn Brooks — whose work reflects a significant change in the focus of black writers. In fiction, black protest had been carried to its pinnacle by Richard Wright in *Uncle Tom's Children* (1938) and *Native Son* (1940). He had not only brought the sound of the ghetto to American critics but had informed them that literature by black writers was competent to be judged according to the criteria used for white writers. From this point on, shrill, sincere protest or naive, humorous exoticism was not sufficient to win laurels for the black writer; he earned distinction only if he mastered his craft.

It is no wonder then that the poets who stand out in the Forties and the Fifties are those who abandoned the old methods and demonstrated their competence in handling the techniques currently in favor among the established critics. Poets who longingly imitated the soft lyricism of John Keats and A. E. Housman were not those who would win praise. Critics looked for traces of T. S. Eliot and Ezra Pound, for free verse, for symbolism, for imagism, for myth and ritual, for experimental syntax.

And they found these new modes and techniques in the work of black writers. The most brilliant, in the opinion of the American critical establishment, was Melvin B. Tolson, who earned accolades from such poets as Robert Frost and Karl Shapiro. Progressing from more conventional protest in his first collection, *Rendezvous with America* (1944), Tolson demonstrated his competence in the Eliot-Pound style in *Libretto for the Republic of Liberia* (1953), which Allen Tate praised for its mastery of "the language of the Anglo-American poetic tradition." Tolson concluded his work with the complex, imaginative, humorous, elusive *Harlem Gallery* (1965), which, Shapiro predicted, would give a new language to American poetry. Starting with a more traditional lyricism in *Heart-Shape in the Dust* (1940), Robert Hayden became progressively symbolic and experimental in his subsequent works, *Figure of Time* (1955) and *A Ballad of Remembrance* (1962). Margaret Walker gave fresh, free expression to black songs of pride in *For My People* (1942). In *Powerful Long Ladder* (1946), Owen Dodson demonstrated the skillful impressionism which characterizes his subsequent novel, *Boy at the Window* (1951). Gwendolyn Brooks achieved recognition as the first Negro author to win a Pulitzer Prize, for *Annie Allen* (1949), a presentation of the mind and emotions of a black woman. In that collection Miss Brooks demonstrated excellent craftsmanship in varying modes from those as old as the ballad to the most recent. In *Montage of a Dream Deferred* (1951), Langston Hughes replaced his jazz and blues with the newer musical idioms of boogie-woogie and bebop, and continued to search for even newer techniques in *Ask Your Mama* (1961).

During the 1960's a new tradition began in black culture — the Black Arts Movement. Inspired by identity and pride derived from black nationalism, young black artists have repudiated the traditions which they identify with the culture of Western Europe. In vestiges of African heritage and in the soul of black ghettoes in America they seek subject-matter, idiom, cadence, and style for art which will inspire black people to liberate themselves from the various forms of bondage — cultural, psychological, spiritual, political, emotional, and economic — which have determined their unequal existence in a society oriented to the values of the white middle-class. Unlike earlier Afro-American protest, it is not a plea for submersion in a melting pot. Instead, it is a demand that black people identify, respect, and free themselves.

The leader of the movement, the most influential black writer since Richard Wright, is LeRoi Jones, who in his first volume, *Preface to a Twenty-Volume Suicide Note* (1961), demonstrated his talent in the more conventional modes. Another respected writer of the decade is Conrad Kent Rivers, who, in his last work, was moving along the path traced by Jones after earlier work — *Perchance to Dream, Othello* (1959) and *These Black Bodies and This Sunburned Face* (1962) — in which he examined his identity. Other voices are too new for a judgment about who will excel. Some of the more promising are Don L. Lee, Etheridge Knight, A. B. Spellman (*The Beautiful Day and Others*, 1964) and Calvin C. Hernton (*The Coming of Chronos to the House of Night Song*, 1964). Many of the younger poets have not yet collected their works. Some are publishing in *Negro Digest, Black Expression* (edited by Don Lee), *Journal of Black Poetry*, and less well-known periodicals. Others are still reading their work to audiences in Newark, Chicago, San Francisco, Brooklyn, and other centers, where college-trained listeners mingle with high school dropouts.

It is dangerous to predict the influence of an artistic revolution which is in its initial stages. Two characteristics, however, are significant. One, the black writers, for the first time in American history, have the advantage of being in the vanguard of an artistic revolt. Now they are the avant-garde writers benefiting from their mutual sharing of ideas. Second, their readings reveal that they are looking back to an oral tradition in which they are perhaps more skilled than their white countrymen. Much of this new poetry depends for its eloquence upon intonation, rhythm, and gesture — qualities which have enriched the folk art of black Americans but which cannot be reproduced adequately in writing. This very strength may conceal its art from those able to approach it only on a printed page. But this fact matters little to the black poets who, indifferent to older and estranged readers, seek to please the new critics who are learning to describe the current work so that they may prescribe for the future. In two hundred years, black singers have moved from folk art dependent on oral presentation, through imitation of obsolescing traditions, through mastery of a present tradition, to a revolutionary art dependent on oral presentation.

Phillis Wheatley (1753?-1784)

Kidnapped from Senegal, West Africa, in the early 1760's, Phillis Wheatley was sold in Boston to John Wheatley, a tailor. After learning to read scriptures within sixteen months, she was encouraged to continue her studies. Within a few years she mastered the education customary for a girl of that time. In 1770, she published her first poem, commemorating the death of a local minister. Three years later, no longer a slave, she published in London *Poems on Various Subjects, Religious and Moral.* After an unhappy marriage with a black man named Peters, she died in 1784.

Imitating the styles of eighteenth-century poetry, especially the style of Alexander Pope, Phillis Wheatley generally wrote tributes, elegies, and lyric poems on noble themes. Judged according to present standards, her poetry is stilted and artificial; but it equals the quality of the work of her fellow Americans in the late eighteenth century. Attention has been called frequently to the absence of racial protest in her work. Richard Wright assumed that the non-racial tone attested to the fact that she was accepted completely within her community. It is equally possible, however, that she did not wish to offend her benevolent master with complaints about her fortune.

The following poems typify her style and thought. In the first two, it is not surprising that she expresses preference for America above her homeland, which was part of dim childhood memories; it is significant, however, that she urges greater respect for the potential of Africans. Her advice to Harvard students was written in 1767. Much longer than her usual lyrics, "Goliath of Gath" is a smooth narration of the familiar Biblical story of David and Goliath.

9

On being brought from Africa to America

'Twas mercy brought me from my *Pagan* land,
Taught my benighted soul to understand
That there's a God, that there's a *Saviour* too:
Once I redemption neither sought nor knew.
Some view our sable race with scornful eye,
"Their colour is a diabolic die."
Remember, *Christians*, *Negros*, black as *Cain*,
May be refin'd, and join th' angelic train.

To the University Of Cambridge, in New-England.

While an intrinsic ardor prompts to write,
The muses promise to assist my pen;
'Twas not long since I left my native shore
The land of errors, and *Egyptian* gloom:
Father of mercy, 'twas thy gracious hand
Brought me in safety from those dark abodes.

　　Students, to you 'tis giv'n to scan the heights
Above, to traverse the ethereal space,
And mark the systems of revolving worlds.
Still more, ye sons of science, ye receive
The blissful news by messengers from heav'n
How *Jesus'* blood for your redemption flows.
See him with hands out-strecht upon the cross;
Immense compassion in his bosom glows;
He hears revilers, nor resents their scorn:
What matchless mercy in the Son of God!
When the whole human race by sin had fall'n,
He deign'd to die that they might rise again,
And share with him in the sublimest skies,
Life without death, and glory without end.

　　Improve your privileges while they stay,
Ye pupils, and each hour redeem, that bears
Or good or bad report of you to heav'n.
Let sin, that baneful evil to the soul,

By you be shunned, nor once remit your guard;
Suppress the deadly serpent in its egg.
Ye blooming plants of human race divine,
An *Ethiop* tells you 'tis your greatest foe;
Its transient sweetness turns to endless pain,
And in immense perdition sinks the soul.

Goliath of Gath
I. Sam. Chap. xvii.

Ye martial pow'rs, and all ye tuneful nine,
Inspire my song, and aid my high design.
The dreadful scenes and toils of war I write,
The ardent warriors, and the fields of fight:
You best remember, and you best can sing
The acts of heroes to the vocal string:
Resume the lays with which your sacred lyre,
Did then the poet and the sage inspire.

Now front to front the armies were display'd,
Here *Israel* rang'd, and there the foes array'd;
The hosts on two opposing mountains stood,
Thick as the foliage of the waving wood;
Between them an extensive valley lay,
O'er which the gleaming armour pour'd the day,
When from the camp of the *Philistine* foes,
Dreadful to view, a mighty warrior rose;
In the dire deeds of bleeding battle skill'd,
The monster stalks the terror of the field.
From *Gath* he sprung, *Goliath* was his name,
Of fierce deportment, and gigantic frame:
A brazen helmet on his head was plac'd,
A coat of mail his form terrific grac'd,
The greaves his legs, the targe his shoulders prest:
Dreadful in arms high-tow'ring o'er the rest
A spear he proudly wav'd, whose iron head,
Strange to relate, six hundred shekels weigh'd;
He strode along and shook the ample field,
While *Phoebus* blaz'd refulgent on his shield:
Through *Jacob's* race a chilling horror ran,
When thus the huge, enormous chief began:

"Say, what the cause that in this proud array
"You set your battle in the face of day?
"One hero find in all your vaunting train,
"Then see who loses, and who wins the plain:
"For he who wins, in triumph may demand
"Perpetual service from the vanquish'd land:
"Your armies I defy, your force despise,
"By far inferior in *Philistia's* eyes:
"Produce a man, and let us try the fight,
"Decide the contest, and the victor's right."

    Thus challeng'd he; all *Israel* stood amaz'd,
And ev'ry chief in consternation gaz'd;
But *Jesse's* son in youthful bloom appears,
And warlike courage far beyond his years:
He left the folds, he left the flow'ry meads,
And soft recesses of the sylvan shades.
Now *Israel's* monarch, and his troops arise, ⎤
With peals of shouts ascending to the skies; ⎬
In *Elah's* vale the scene of combat lies,   ⎦

    When the fair morning blush'd with orient red,
What *David's* sire enjoin'd the son obey'd,
And swift of foot towards the trench he came,
Where glow'd each bosom with the martial flame.
He leaves his carriage to another's care,
And runs to greet his brethren of the war.
While yet they spake the giant-chief arose,
Repeats the challenge, and insults his foes:
Struck with the sound, and trembling at the view,
Affrighted *Israel* from its post withdrew.
"Observe ye this tremendous foe, they cry'd,
"Who in proud vaunts our armies hath defy'd:
"Whoever lays him prostrate on the plain,
"Freedom in *Israel* for his house shall gain;
"And on him wealth unknown the king will pour,
"And give his royal daughter for his dow'r."

    Then *Jesse's* youngest hope: "My brethren say,
"What shall be done for him who takes away
"Reproach from *Jacob*, who destroys the chief,
"And puts a period to his country's grief.

"He vaunts the honours of his arms abroad,
"And scorns the armies of the living God."

    Thus spoke the youth, th' attentive people ey'd
The wond'rous hero, and again reply'd:
"Such the rewards our monarch will bestow,
"On him who conquers, and destroys his foe,"

    Eliab heard, and kindled into ire
To hear his shepherd brother thus inquire,
And thus begun? "What errand brought thee? say
"Who keeps thy flock? or does it go astray?
"I know the base ambition of thine heart,
"But back in safety from the field depart,"

    Eliab thus to *Jesse's* youngest heir,
Express'd his wrath in accents most severe.
When to his brother mildly he reply'd,
"What have I done? or what the cause to chide?"

    The words were told before the king, who sent
For the young hero to his royal tent:
Before the monarch dauntless he began,
"For this *Philistine* fail no heart of man:
"I'll take the vale, and with the giant fight:
"I dread not all his boasts, nor all his might."
When thus the king: "Dar'st thou a stripling go,
"And venture combat with so great a foe?
"Who all his days has been inur'd to fight,
"And made its deeds his study and delight:
"Battles and bloodshed brought the monster forth,
"And clouds and whirlwinds usher'd in his birth."
When David thus: "I kept the fleecy care,
"And out there rush'd a lion and a bear;
"A tender lamb the hungry lion took,
"And with no other weapon than my crook
"Bold I pursu'd, and chas'd him o'er the field,
"The prey deliver'd, and the felon kill'd:
"As thus the lion and the bear I slew,
"So shall *Goliath* fall, and all his crew:
"The God, who sav'd me from these beasts of prey,
"By me this monster in the dust shall lay."

So *David* spoke: "The wond'ring king reply'd;
"Go thou with heav'n and victory on thy side;
"This coat of mail, this sword gird on," he said,
And plac'd a mighty helmet on his head:
The coat, the sword, the helm he laid aside,
Nor chose to venture with those arms untry'd,
Then took his staff, and to the neighb'ring brook
Instant he ran, and thence five pebbles took,
Mean time descended to *Philistia's* son
A radiant cherub, and he thus begun:
"*Goliath*, well thou know'st thou hast defy'd
"Yon Hebrew armies, and their God deny'd:
"Rebellious wretch! audacious worm! forbear,
"Nor tempt the vengeance of their God too far:
"Them, who with his omnipotence contend,
"No eye shall pity, and no arm defend:
"Proud as thou art, in short liv'd glory great,
"I come to tell thee thine approaching fate.
"Regard my words. The judge of all the gods,
"Beneath whose steps the tow'ring mountain nods,
"Will give thine armies to the savage brood,
"That cut the liquid air, or range the wood.
"Thee too a well-aim'd pebble shall destroy,
"And thou shalt perish by a beardless boy:
"Such is the mandate from the realms above, ⎫
"And should I try the vengeance to remove, ⎬
"Myself a rebel to my king would prove. ⎭
"*Goliath* say, shall grace to him be shown,
"Who dares heav'ns monarch, and insults his throne?"

   "Your words are lost on me," the giant cries, ⎫
While fear and wrath contended in his eyes, ⎬
When thus the messenger from heav'n replies: ⎭
"Provoke no more *Jehovah's* awful hand
"To hurl its vengeance on thy guilty land:
"He grasps the thunder, and, he wings the storm,
"Servants their sov'reign's orders to perform."
The angel spoke, and turn'd his eyes away,
Adding new radiance to the rising day.

   Now *David* comes. The fatal stones demand
His left, the staff engag'd his better hand:
The giant mov'd, and from his tow'ring height

Survey'd the stripling, and disdain'd the fight,
And thus began: "Am I a dog with thee?
"Bring'st thou no amour, but a staff to me?
"The gods on thee their vollied curses pour,
"And beasts and birds of prey thy flesh devour,"

    David undaunted thus, "Thy spear and shield
"Shall no protection to thy body yield:
"*Jehovah's* name — — no other arms I bear,
"I ask no other in this glorious war.
"To-day the Lord of Hosts to me will give
"Vict'ry, to-day thy doom thou shalt receive;
"The fate you threaten shall your own become,
"And beasts shall be your animated tomb,
"That all the earth's inhabitants may know
"That there's a God, who governs all below:
"This great assembly too shall witness stand,
"That needs nor sword, nor spear, th' Almighty's hand:
"The battle his, the conquest he bestows,
"And to our pow'r consigns our hated foes."

    Thus *David* spoke; *Goliath* heard and came
To meet the hero in the field of fame.
Ah! fatal meeting to thy troops and thee,
But thou wast deaf to the divine decree;
Young *David* meets thee, meets thee not in vain;
'Tis thine to perish on th' ensanguin'd plain.

    And now the youth the forceful pebble flung,
Philistia trembled as it whizz'd along:
In his dread forehead, where the helmet ends,
Just o'er the brows the well-aim'd stone descends,
It pierc'd the skull, and shatter'd all the brain,
Prone on his face he tumbled to the plain:
Goliath's fall no smaller terror yields
Than riving thunders in aerial fields:
The soul still ling'red in its lov'd abode,
Till conq'ring *David* o'er the giant strode:
Goliath's sword then laid its master dead,
And from the body hew'd the ghastly head;
The blood in gushing torrents drench'd the plains,
The soul found passage through the spouting veins.

And now aloud the illustrious victor said,
"Where are your boastings now your champion's dead?"
Scarce had he spoke when the *Philistines* fled:
But fled in vain; the conqu'ror swift pursu'd:
What scenes of slaughter! and what seas of blood!
There *Saul* thy thousands grasp'd th' impurpled sand
In pangs of death the conquest of thine hand;
And *David* there were thy ten thousands laid:
Thus *Israel's* damsels musically play'd.
   Near *Gath* and *Ekron* many an hero lay,
Breath'd out their souls, and curs'd the light of day;
Their fury quench'd by death, no longer burns,
And *David* with *Goliath's* head returns,
To *Salem* brought, but in his tent he plac'd
The load of armour which the giant grac'd,
His monarch saw him coming from the war,
And thus demanded of the son of *Ner*.
"Say, who is this amazing youth?" he cry'd,
When thus the leader of the host reply'd;
"As lives thy soul I know not whence he sprung,
"So great in prowess though in years so young:"
"Inquire whose son is he," the sov'reign said,
"Before whose conq'ring arm *Philistia* fled."
Before the king behold the stripling stand,
Goliath's head depending from his hand:
To him the king: "Say of what martial line
"Art thou, young hero, and what sire was thine?"
He humbly thus: "The son of *Jesse* I:
"I came the glories of the field to try,
"Small is my tribe, but valiant in the fight;
"Small is my city, but thy royal right."
"Then take the promis'd gifts," the monarch cry'd,
Conferring riches and the royal bride;
"Knit to my soul for ever thou remain
"With me, nor quit my regal roof again."

George Moses Horton
(1797-1883)

A slave in Northhampton County, North Carolina, George Moses Horton was a black Cyrano for hundreds of male students at the University of North Carolina at Chapel Hill, who commissioned him to write love lyrics to their sweethearts. Although Horton's poetry is not distinguished by protests against slavery, the cry for liberty occasionally appears, particularly in *The Hope of Liberty* (1829), from which he hoped to earn enough money to purchase his freedom. Even a reprinting of this volume, as *Poems by a Slave* (1837), failed to raise the required sum; therefore, Horton remained a slave until 1865, when he was freed by the Union troops. In the same year he published his final collection, *Naked Genius*.

The following reveal Horton's characteristic themes of conventional moralizing, appreciation of nature, and sentimentalizing of love.

The Swan — Vain Pleasures

The Swan which boasted mid the tide,
Whose nest was guarded by the wave,
Floated for pleasure till she died,
And sunk beneath the flood to lave.

The bird of fashion drops her wing,
The rose-bush now declines to bloom;
The gentle breezes of the spring
No longer waft a sweet perfume.

Fair beauty with those lovely eyes,
Withers along her vital stream;
Proud fortune leaves her throne, and flies
From pleasure, as a flattering dream.

17

The eagle of exalted fame,
Which spreads his pinions far to sail,
Struggled to fan his dying flame,
Till pleasure pall'd in every gale.

And gaudy mammon, sordid gain,
Whose plume has faded, once so gay,
Languishes mid the flowery train,
Whilst pleasure flies like fumes away.

Vain pleasures, O how short to last!
Like leaves which quick to ashes burn;
Which kindle from the slightest blast,
And slight to nothing hence return.

The Powers of Love

It lifts the poor man from his cell
    To fortune's bright alcove;
Its mighty sway few, few can tell,
Mid envious foes it conquers ill;
    There's nothing half like love.

Ye weary strangers, void of rest,
    Who late through life have strove,
Like the late bird which seeks its nest,
If you would hence in truth be blest,
    Light on the bough of love.

The vagrant plebeian, void of friends,
    Constrain'd through wilds to rove,
On this his safety whole depends,
One faithful smile his trouble ends,
    A smile of constant love.

Thus did a captured wretch complain,
    Imploring heaven above,
Till one with sympathetic pain,
Flew to his arms and broke the chain,
    And grief took flight from love.

Let clouds of danger rise and roar,
  And hope's firm pillars move,
With storms behind and death before,
O grant me this, I crave no more,
  There's nothing half like love.

When nature wakes soft pity's coo
  The hawk deserts the dove,
Compassion melts the creature through,
With palpitations felt by few,
  The wrecking throbs of love.

Let surly discord take its flight
  From wedlock's peaceful grove,
While union breaks the arm of fight,
With darkness swallow'd up in light,
  O what is there like love.

To a Departing Favorite

Thou mayst retire, but think of me
  When thou art gone afar,
Where'er in life thy travels be,
If tost along the brackish sea,
  Or borne upon the car.

Thou mayst retire, I care not where,
  Thy name my theme shall be;
With thee in heart I shall be there,
Content thy good or ill to share,
  If dead to lodge with thee.

Thou mayst retire beyond the deep,
  And leave thy sister train,
To roam the wilds where dangers sleep,
And leave affection sad to weep
  In bitterness and pain.

Thou mayst retire, and yet be glad
  To leave me thus alone,
Lamenting and bewailing sad;
Farewell, thy sunk deluded lad
  May rise when thou art gone.

The Eye of Love

I know her story-telling eye
    Has more expression than her tongue;
And from that heart-extorted sigh,
    At once the peal of love is rung.

When that soft eye lets fall a tear
    Of doating fondness as we part,
The stream is from a cause sincere,
    And issues from a melting heart.

What shall her fluttering pulse restrain,
    The life-watch beating from her soul,
When all the power of hate is slain,
    And love permits it no control.

When said her tongue, I wish thee well,
    Her eye declared it must be true;
And every sentence seem'd to tell
    The tale of sorrow told by few.

When low she bow'd and wheel'd aside,
    I saw her blushing temples fade;
Her smiles were sunk in sorrow's tide,
    But love was in her eye betray'd.

The Setting Sun

'Tis sweet to trace the setting sun
    Wheel blushing down the west;
When his diurnal race is run,
The traveller stops the gloom to shun,
    And lodge his bones to rest.

Far from the eye he sinks apace,
    But still throws back his light
From oceans of resplendant grace,
Whence sleeping vesper paints her face,
    And bids the sun good night.

To those hesperian fields by night
  My thoughts in vision stray,
Like spirits stealing into light,
From gloom upon the wing of flight,
  Soaring from time away.

Our eagle, with his pinions furl'd,
  Takes his departing peep,
And hails the occidental world,
Swift round whose base the globes are whirl'd,
  Whilst weary creatures sleep.

Paul Laurence Dunbar
(1872-1906)

Born in Dayton, Ohio, Paul Laurence Dunbar, the son of former slaves, became one of the most popular American poets of his time. Although he published his first collection, *Oak and Ivy*, in 1892 while working as an elevator operator, Dunbar did not gain national attention until William Dean Howells favorably reviewed *Majors and Minors* (1896) and followed with a laudatory introduction to *Lyrics of Lowly Life* (1896), in which he described Dunbar as the first American Negro to "evince innate artistic talent." Despite poor health Dunbar published three additional collections of original poems: *Lyrics of the Hearthside* (1899), *Lyrics of Love and Laughter* (1903), and *Lyrics of Sunshine and Shadow* (1905).

Although he wrote four novels and four collections of stories, Paul Laurence Dunbar should be remembered as a poet rather than a writer of fiction. Because he is known best as a writer of comic or sentimental monologues in Negro dialect, modern readers have overlooked his conscious artistry and experimentation with meter and rhyme, his skillful imitations of the dialects of Caucasian inhabitants of Ohio and Indiana, his many tributes to Afro-American heroes, the characteristic melancholy of much of his standard-English poetry, and the fact that he wrote more poetry in standard English than in dialect. Nevertheless, his chief talents — rhythm, narrative skill, and satirical characterization — are best revealed in his dialect poems, his major contribution to American literature.

The first two of the following selections illustrate Dunbar's eloquent tributes to Afro-American heroes and ancestry. The third selection is one of Dunbar's earliest and most highly praised meditations. The fourth, in Negro dialect, reveals Dunbar's humor, the characteristic rhythm which he developed for these monologues, and his understanding of the indirect protests of slaves. The final selection exhibits both the charm of Dunbar's many poems about children and his imitation of non-Negro dialect.

23

Frederick Douglass

A hush is over all the teeming lists,
    And there is pause, a breath-space in the strife;
A spirit brave has passed beyond the mists
    And vapors that obscure the sun of life.
And Ethiopia, with bosom torn,
Laments the passing of her noblest born.

She weeps for him a mother's burning tears —
    She loved him with a mother's deepest love.
He was her champion thro' direful years,
    And held her weal all other ends above.
When Bondage held her bleeding in the dust,
He raised her up and whispered, "Hope and Trust."

For her his voice, a fearless clarion, rung
    That broke in warning on the ears of men;
For her the strong bow of his power he strung,
    And sent his arrows to the very den
Where grim Oppression held his bloody place
And gloated o'er the mis'ries of a race.

And he was no soft-tongued apologist;
    He spoke straightforward, fearlessly uncowed;
The sunlight of his truth dispelled the mist,
    And set in bold relief each dark-hued cloud;
To sin and crime he gave their proper hue,
And hurled at evil what was evil's due.

Through good and ill report he cleaved his way
    Right onward, with his face set toward the heights,
Nor feared to face the foeman's dread array, —
    The lash of scorn, the sting of petty spites.
He dared the lightning in the lightning's track,
And answered thunder with his thunder back.

Ode to Ethiopia

O Mother Race! to thee I bring
This pledge of faith unwavering,
    This tribute to thy glory.

I know the pangs which thou didst feel,
When Slavery crushed thee with its heel,
　With thy dear blood all gory.

Sad days were those — ah, sad indeed!
But through the land the fruitful seed
　Of better times was growing.
The plant of freedom upward sprung,
And spread its leaves so fresh and young —
　Its blossoms now are blowing.

On every hand in this fair land,
Proud Ethiope's swarthy children stand
　Beside their fairer neighbor;
The forests flee before their stroke,
Their hammers ring, their forges smoke, —
　They stir in honest labour.

They tread the fields where honour calls;
Their voices sound through senate halls
　In majesty and power.
To right they cling; the hymns they sing
Up to the skies in beauty ring,
　And bolder grow each hour.

Be proud, my Race, in mind and soul;
Thy name is writ on Glory's scroll
　In characters of fire.
High 'mid the clouds of Fame's bright sky
Thy banner's blazoned folds now fly,
　And truth shall lift them higher.

Thou hast the right to noble pride,
Whose spotless robes were purified
　By blood's severe baptism.
Upon thy brow the cross was laid,
And labour's painful sweat-beads made
　A consecrating chrism.

No other race, or white or black,
When bound as thou wert, to the rack,
　So seldom stooped to grieving;

No other race, when free again,
Forgot the past and proved them men
    So noble in forgiving.

Go on and up! Our souls and eyes
Shall follow thy continuous rise;
    Our ears shall list thy story
From bards who from thy root shall spring,
And proudly tune their lyres to sing
    Of Ethiopia's glory.

Ere Sleep Comes Down to
Soothe the Weary Eyes

Ere sleep comes down to soothe the weary eyes,
    Which all the day with ceaseless care have sought
The magic gold which from the seeker flies;
    Ere dreams put on the gown and cap of thought,
And make the waking world a world of lies, —
    Of lies most palpable, uncouth, forlorn,
That say life's full of aches and tears and sighs, —
    Oh, how with more than dreams the soul is torn,
Ere sleep comes down to soothe the weary eyes.

Ere sleep comes down to soothe the weary eyes,
    How all the griefs and heartaches we have known
Come up like pois'nous vapors that arise
    From some base witch's caldron, when the crone,
To work some potent spell, her magic plies.
    The past which held its share of bitter pain,
Whose ghost we prayed that Time might exorcise,
    Comes up, is lived and suffered o'er again,
Ere sleep comes down to soothe the weary eyes.

Ere sleep comes down to soothe the weary eyes,
    What phantoms fill the dimly lighted room;
What ghostly shades in awe-creating guise
    Are bodied forth within the teeming gloom.
What echoes faint of sad and soul-sick cries,
    And pangs of vague inexplicable pain

That pay the spirit's ceaseless enterprise,
　　Come thronging through the chambers of the brain,
Ere sleep comes down to soothe the weary eyes.

Ere sleep comes down to soothe the weary eyes,
　　Where ranges forth the spirit far and free?
Through what strange realms and unfamiliar skies
　　Tends her far course to lands of mystery?
To lands unspeakable — beyond surmise,
　　Where shapes unknowable to being spring,
Till, faint of wing, the Fancy fails and dies
　　Much wearied with the spirit's journeying,
Ere sleep comes down to soothe the weary eyes.

Ere sleep comes down to soothe the weary eyes,
　　How questioneth the soul that other soul, —
The inner sense which neither cheats nor lies,
　　But self exposes unto self, a scroll
Full writ with all life's acts unwise or wise,
　　In characters indelible and known;
So, trembling with the shock of sad surprise,
　　The soul doth view its awful self alone,
Ere sleep comes down to soothe the weary eyes.

When sleep comes down to seal the weary eyes,
　　The last dear sleep whose soft embrace is balm,
And whom sad sorrow teaches us to prize
　　For kissing all our passions into calm,
Ah, then, no more we heed the sad world's cries,
　　Or seek to probe th' eternal mystery,
Or fret our souls at long-withheld replies,
　　At glooms through which our visions cannot see,
When sleep comes down to seal the weary eyes.

An Ante-Bellum Sermon

We is gathahed hyeah, my brothahs,
　　In dis howlin' wildaness,
Fu' to speak some words of comfo't
　　To each othah in distress.

An' we chooses fu' ouah subjic'
  Dis — we'll 'splain it by an' by;
"An' de Lawd said, 'Moses, Moses,'
  An' de man said, 'Hyeah am I.' "

Now ole Pher'oh, down in Egypt,
  Was de wuss man evah bo'n,
An' he had de Hebrew chillun
  Down dah wukin' in his co'n;
'T well de Lawd got tiahed o' his foolin',
  An' sez he: "I'll let him know —
Look hyeah, Moses, go tell Pher'oh
  Fu' to let dem chillun go."

"An' ef he refuse to do it,
  I will make him rue de houah,
Fu' I'll empty down on Egypt
  All de vials of my powah."
Yes, he did — an' Pher'oh's ahmy
  Was n't wuth a ha'f a dime;
Fu' de Lawd will he'p his chillun,
  You kin trust him evah time.

An' yo' enemies may 'sail you
  In de back an' in de front;
But de Lawd is all aroun' you,
  Fu' to ba' de battle's brunt.
Dey kin fo'ge yo' chains an' shackles
  F'om de mountains to de sea;
But de Lawd will sen' some Moses
  Fu' to set his chillun free.

An' de lan' shall hyeah his thundah,
  Lak a blas' f'om Gab'el's ho'n,
Fu' de Lawd of hosts is mighty
  When he girds his ahmor on.
But fu' feah some one mistakes me,
  I will pause right hyeah to say,
Dat I'm still a-preachin' ancient,
  I ain't talkin' 'bout to-day.

But I tell you, fellah christuns,
    Things 'll happen mighty strange;
Now, de Lawd done dis fu' Isrul,
    An' his ways don't nevah change,
An' de love he showed to Isrul
    Was n't all on Isrul spent;
Now don't run an' tell yo' mastahs
    Dat I's preachin' discontent.

'Cause I is n't; I'se a-judgin'
    Bible people by deir ac's;
I'se a-givin' you de Scriptuah,
    I'se a-handin' you de fac's.
Cose ole Pher'oh b'lieved in slav'ry
    But de Lawd he let him see,
Dat de people he put bref in, —
    Evah mothah's son was free.

An' dahs othahs thinks lak Pher'oh,
    But dey calls de Scriptuah liar,
Fu' de Bible says "a servant
    Is a-worthy of his hire."
An' you cain't git roun' nor thoo dat,
    An' you cain't git ovah it,
Fu' whatevah place you git in,
    Dis hyeah Bible too 'll fit.

So you see de Lawd's intention,
    Evah sence de worl' began,
Was dat His almighty freedom
    Should belong to evah man,
But I think it would be bettah,
    Ef I'd pause agin to say,
Dat I'm talkin' 'bout ouah freedom
    In a Bibleistic way.

But de Moses is a-comin',
    An' he's comin', suah and fas'
We kin hyeah his feet a-trompin',
    We kin hyeah his trumpit blas'.

But I want to wa'n you people,
  Don't you git too brigity;
An' don't you git to braggin'
  'Bout dese things, you wait an' see.

But when Moses wif his powah
  Comes an' sets us chillun free,
We will praise de gracious Mastah
  Dat has gin us liberty;
An' we'll shout ouah halleluyahs,
  On dat mighty reck'nin' day,
When we'se reco'nised ez citiz' —
  Huh uh! Chillun, let us pray!

When a Feller's Itchin' to be Spanked

W'en us fellers stomp around, makin' lots o' noise,
Gramma says, "There's certain times comes to little boys
W'en they need a shingle or the soft side of a plank;"
She says "we're a-itchin' for a right good spank."
  An' she says, "Now thes you wait,
    It's a-comin' — soon or late,
  W'en a fellers itchin' fer a spank."

W'en a feller's out o' school, you know how he feels,
Gramma says we wriggle 'roun like a lot o' eels.
W'y it's like a man that's thes home from out o' jail.
What's the use o' scoldin' if we pull Tray's tail?
  Gramma says, tho', "thes you wait,
    It's a-comin' — soon or late,
  You'se the boys that's itchin' to be spanked."

Cats is funny creatures an' I like to make 'em yowl,
Gramma alwus looks at me with a awful scowl
An' she says, "Young gentlemen, mamma should be thanked
Ef you'd get your knickerbockers right well spanked."
  An' she says, "Now thes you wait,
    It's a-comin' — soon or late,"
  W'en a feller's itchin' to be spanked.

Ef you fin' the days is gettin' awful hot in school
An' you know a swimmin' place where it's nice and cool,
Er you know a cat-fish hole brimmin' full o' fish,
Whose a-goin' to set around school and wish?
   'Tain't no use to hide your bait,
    It's a-comin' — soon or late,
W'en a feller's itchin' to be spanked.

Ol' folks know most ever-thing 'bout the world, I guess,
Gramma does, we wish she knowed thes a little less,
But I alwus kind o' think it 'ud be as well
Ef they wouldn't alwus have to up an' tell;
   We kids wish 'at they'd thes wait,
    It's a-comin' — soon or late,
W'en a feller's itchin' to be spanked.

W[illiam] S[tanley] Braithwaite (1878-1961)

W.S. Braithwaite, of West Indian ancestry, was born and reared in Boston, Massachusetts. Although he worked several years on the editorial staff of the Boston *Transcript* and served as Professor of Creative Literature at Atlanta University, Braithwaite is remembered more widely as an anthologist and a poet. From 1913 to 1929 he edited an annual anthology of magazine verse, in which he included early works of such important poets as Vachel Lindsay and Carl Sandburg. He also edited anthologies of Restoration, Georgian, and Victorian verse.

As a critic, he encouraged experimental poets. But in his own writing — collected in *Lyrics of Life and Love* (1904), *The House of Falling Leaves* (1908), and *Selected Poems* (1948), he imitated the traditions of nineteenth-century lyric poetry and wrote chiefly on non-racial themes, as is evidenced in the following selections.

Rhapsody

I am glad daylong for the gift of song,
   For time and change and sorrow;
For the sunset wings and the world-end things
   Which hang on the edge of to-morrow.
I am glad for my heart whose gates apart
   Are the entrance-place of wonders,
Where dreams come in from the rush and din
   Like sheep from the rains and thunders.

To———

Half in the dim light from the hall
I saw your fingers rise and fall
Along the pale, dusk-shadowed keys,
And heard your subtle melodies.

The magic of your mastery leant
Your soul unto the instrument;
Strange-wise, its spell of power seemed
To voice the visions that you dreamed.

The music gave my soul such wings
As bore me through the shadowings
Of mortal bondage; flight on flight
I circled dreams' supremest height.

Above were tender twilight skies,
Where stars were dreams and memories —
The long forgotten raptures of
My youth's dead fires of hope and love.

If I Could Touch

If I could touch your hand to-night
   And hear you speak one little word,
I then might understand your flight
   Up the star steps, unseen, unheard.

If through the mists of gold and gray
   That tint the weary sunset skies,
There shone two stars across the bay
   That thrilled me like your passionate eyes —

If only some small part of you
   Would speak, or touch, or rise in sight,
Death would be then between us two
   The passing of a summer's night.

Hymn for the Slain in Battle

Lord, God of all in Life and Death,
The winter's storm, the summer's breath,
Of fragrant bloom, — whose Mighty hand
Decrees the pow'r of sea and land,
Hear, Lord, this prayer for those who are
Slain in the hour of thund'rous war.
Have mercy, Lord, on those who fall
Rent by the iron-splintered ball.
Reck not their cause was right or wrong,
'Twas Duty led them blind and strong.
They shaped not what to war gave rise —
They make the greatest sacrifice.

Two Questions

Heart of the soft, wild rose
Hid in a forest close
Far from the world away,
Sweet for a night and day.
Rose, is it good to be sweet,
Sun and the dews to greet?

Life that is mine to keep
In travail, play and sleep
Firm on a tossing ball,
Drilled to march at a call;
Work, love, death — these three —
Life, is there more for me?

James Weldon Johnson
(1871-1938)

A man of diverse talents, James Weldon Johnson, at various times, was a public school teacher, a principal, a lawyer, a leading song writer, a consul for the United States, a novelist, secretary of the National Association for the Advancement of Colored People, a poet, an anthologist, and a college professor. Born in Jacksonville, Florida, he earned a bachelor's degree from Atlanta University. After passing the examination permitting him to practice law in Florida, Johnson, then a high school principal, left both law and education to join his brother Rosamond in New York, where, for several years, the two collaborated in writing successful musical comedies presented on Broadway. From 1906 to 1913 he served as Consul in Venezuela and Nicaragua. After leaving government service, he took a position first as field secretary, later as general secretary for the National Association for the Advancement of Colored People, with which he worked from 1916 to 1930. While a professor at Fisk University, whose faculty he joined in 1930, Johnson was killed in an automobile accident.

Johnson's contributions to black literature are equally varied and impressive. In 1912 he wrote *The Autobiography of an Ex-Coloured Man*, which some critics describe as the most artistic novel by an American Negro prior to the 1920's. In 1922 he edited *The Book of American Negro Poetry* (revised and enlarged in 1931), the first anthology of poetry by black Americans. He also co-edited *The Book of Negro Spirituals* (1925, 1926, 1940). His *Black Manhattan* (1930) is an interesting, highly informative social and cultural history of Afro-Americans in New York. His song, "Lift Every Voice and Sing," was accepted for many years as a national anthem for Negro Americans.

In his early lyrics, written on the traditional themes of musical comedy, Johnson generally used dialect to comply with the images which audiences expected from the Negro characters. "Sence You

37

Went Away" illustrates this practice. When he attempted the more serious task of writing verse sermons, however, Johnson rejected dialect. He feared that dialect supported only comic or pathetic scenes and evoked laughter or pity from readers and audiences. In *God's Trombones: Seven Old-Time Negro Sermons in Verse*, from which "The Creation" is taken, Johnson wished to suggest the nobility as well as the emotional fervor of the sermons of Negro preachers. He believed that, rather than lending realism, dialect would merely distract the reader from the major theme.

Sence You Went Away

Seems lak to me de stars don't shine so bright,
Seems lak to me de sun done loss his light,
Seems lak to me der's nothin' goin' right,
 Sence you went away.

Seems lak to me de sky ain't half so blue,
Seems lak to me dat ev'ything wants you,
Seems lak to me I don't know what to do,
 Sence you went away.

Seems lak to me dat ev'ything is wrong,
Seems lak to me de day's jes twice es long,
Seems lak to me de bird's forgot his song,
 Sence you went away.

Seems lak to me I jes can't he'p but sigh,
Seems lak to me ma th'oat keeps gittin' dry,
Seems lak to me a tear stays in ma eye,
 Sence you went away.

The Creation

And God stepped out on space,
And he looked around and said:
I'm lonely —
I'll make me a world.

And far as the eye of God could see
Darkness covered everything,
Blacker than a hundred midnights
Down in a cypress swamp.

Then God smiled,
And the light broke,
And the darkness rolled up on one side,
And the light stood shining on the other,
And God said: That's good!

Then God reached out and took the light in his hands,
And God rolled the light around in his hands
Until he made the sun;
And he set that sun a-blazing in the heavens.
And the light that was left from making the sun
God gathered it up in a shining ball
And flung it against the darkness,
Spangling the night with the moon and stars.
Then down between
The darkness and the light
He hurled the world;
And God said: That's good!

Then God himself stepped down —
And the sun was on his right hand,
And the moon was on his left;
The stars were clustered about his head,
And the earth was under his feet.
And God walked, and where he trod
His footsteps hollowed the valleys out
And bulged the mountains up.

Then he stopped and looked and saw
That the earth was hot and barren.
So God stepped over to the edge of the world
And he spat out the seven seas —
He batted his eyes, and the lightnings flashed —
He clapped his hands, and the thunders rolled —
And the waters above the earth came down,
The cooling waters came down.

Then the green grass sprouted,
And the little red flowers blossomed,
The pine tree pointed his finger to the sky,
And the oak spread out his arms,
The lakes cuddled down in the hollows of the ground,
And the rivers ran down to the sea;
And God smiled again,
And the rainbow appeared,
And curled itself around his shoulder.

Then God raised his arm and he waved his hand
Over the sea and over the land,
And he said: Bring forth! Bring forth!
And quicker than God could drop his hand,
Fishes and fowls
And beasts and birds
Swam the rivers and the seas,
Roamed the forests and the woods,
And split the air with their wings.
And God said: That's good!

Then God walked around,
And God looked around
On all that he had made.
He looked at his sun,
And he looked at his moon,
And he looked at his little stars;
He looked on his world
With all its living things,
And God said: I'm lonely still.

Then God sat down —
On the side of a hill where he could think;
By a deep, wide river he sat down;
With his head in his hands,
God thought and thought,
Till he thought: I'll make me a man!

Up from the bed of the river
God scooped the clay;
And by the bank of the river
He kneeled him down;

And there the great God Almighty
Who lit the sun and fixed it in the sky,
Who flung the stars to the most far corner of the night,
Who rounded the earth in the middle of his hand;
This Great God,
Like a mammy bending over her baby,
Kneeled down in the dust
Toiling over a lump of clay
Till he shaped it in his own image;

Then into it he blew the breath of life,
And man became a living soul.
Amen. Amen.

Georgia Douglas Johnson
(1886-   )

Born in Atlanta, Georgia, and educated at Atlanta University and Oberlin Conservatory in Ohio, Georgia Douglas Johnson is probably the best-known female Afro-American poet of the several between Frances E. W. Harper, whose last poems were published in 1872, and Margaret Walker, whose collection appeared in 1942. She wrote four volumes of poems: *The Heart of a Woman and Other Poems* (1918), *Bronze: A Book of Verse* (1922), *An Autumn Love Cycle* (1928), and *Share My World* (1962). Although her first book appeared only shortly before the Harlem Renaissance, it is difficult to identify her with that decade of colorful, frequently exotic literature. Despite her treatment of themes of racial identity and social protest, her lyrics are characterized by a quietness and a simplicity evocative of an earlier age.

Black Woman

Don't knock at my door, little child,
   I cannot let you in,
You know not what a world this is
   Of cruelty and sin.
Wait in the still eternity
   Until I come to you,
The world is cruel, cruel, child,
   I cannot let you in!

Don't knock at my door, little one,
   I cannot bear the pain
Of turning deaf-ear to your call
   Time and time again!

43

You do not know the monster men
Inhabiting the earth,
Be still, be still, my precious child,
I must not give you birth!

Credo

I believe in the ultimate justice of Fate;
That the races of men front the sun in their turn;
That each soul holds the title to infinite wealth
In fee to the will as it masters itself;
That the heart of humanity sounds the same tone
In impious jungle, or sky-kneeling fane.
I believe that the key to the life-mystery
Lies deeper than reason and further than death.
I believe that the rhythmical conscience within
Is guidance enough for the conduct of men.

The Suppliant

Long have I beat with timid hands upon life's leaden door,
Praying the patient, futile prayer my fathers prayed before,
Yet I remain without the close, unheeded and unheard,
And never to my listening ear is borne the waited word.

Soft o'er the threshold of the years there comes this counsel cool:
The strong demand, contend, prevail; the beggar is a fool!

To William Stanley Braithwaite

When time has rocked the present age to sleep,
And lighter hearts are lilting to the sway
Of rhythmic poesy's enhanced lay,
Recurring sequences shall fitly keep
Your fame eternal, as they lightly sweep
Aside the curtain to that potent day
When you in primal fervor led the way
Unto Apollo's narrow winding steep.

None shall forget your travail, utter, sore,
That oped the golden avenue of song,
When, like a knight, so errantly you bore
The mantled children valiantly along,
Their homage as a rising incense sweet
Shall permeate the heavens at your feet!

Claude McKay (1891-1948)

Although he was born in Jamaica, British West Indies, where he published his first book of poems, *Songs of Jamaica* (1911), Claude McKay is identified with the Harlem Renaissance of the 1920's. Arriving in the United States in 1912, he studied at Tuskegee Institute and Kansas State University. In 1920 he became associate editor of *The Liberator*, and in 1922 he published *Harlem Shadows*, his third collection of poems but the first issued in the United States.

Today McKay is probably best-known for such novels as *Home to Harlem* (1928) and *Banjo* (1929). He was perhaps even more talented as a poet. His poems are colorful, evocative, and powerful, whether he was writing nostalgically about his boyhood or bitterly about the rejection and the abuse of black Americans.

"If We Must Die," one of the following selections, has an ironic history. During World War II, Prime Minister Winston Churchill read this poem publicly to encourage supporters of democracy in what, at that time, seemed an almost hopeless war against Fascists. Claude McKay, however, had written the poem in reaction to a massacre of Afro-Americans in the United States.

The other selections offer a medley of themes characterizing McKay's work: feeling of alienation and loss of ancestral identity, hatred of an oppressive land, interest in Africa, admiration for America, protest against white Americans' abuse of black Americans, nostalgia for Jamaica, compassion for the ordinary people of Harlem, and love.

Outcast

For the dim regions whence my fathers came
My spirit, bondaged by the body, longs.
Words felt, but never heard, my lips would frame;

47

My soul would sing forgotten jungle songs.
I would go back to darkness and to peace,
But the great western world holds me in fee,
And I may never hope for full release
While to its alien gods I bend my knee.
Something in me is lost, forever lost,
Some vital thing has gone out of my heart,
And I must walk the way of life a ghost
Among the sons of earth, a thing apart;
For I was born, far from my native clime,
Under the white man's menace, out of time.

Enslaved

Oh when I think of my long-suffering race,
For weary centuries despised, oppressed,
Enslaved and lynched, denied a human place
In the great life line of the Christian West;
And in the Black Land disinherited,
Robbed in the ancient country of its birth,
My heart grows sick with hate, becomes as lead,
For this my race that has no home on earth.
Then from the dark depths of my soul I cry
To the avenging angel to consume
The white man's world of wonders utterly:
Let it be swallowed up in earth's vast womb,
Or upward roll as sacrificial smoke
To liberate my people from its yoke!

Africa

The sun sought thy dim bed and brought forth light,
The sciences were sucklings at thy breast;
When all the world was young in pregnant night
Thy slaves toiled at thy monumental best.
Thou ancient treasure-land, thou modern prize,
New peoples marvel at thy pyramids!
The years roll on, thy sphinx of riddle eyes
Watches the mad world with immobile lids.
The Hebrews humbled them at Pharaoh's name.

Cradle of Power! Yet all things were in vain!
Honor and Glory, Arrogance and Fame!
They went. The darkness swallowed thee again.
Thou art the harlot, now thy time is done,
Of all the mighty nations of the sun.

America

Although she feeds me bread of bitterness,
And sinks into my throat her tiger's tooth,
Stealing my breath of life, I will confess
I love this cultured hell that tests my youth!
Her vigor flows like tides into my blood,
Giving me strength erect against her hate.
Her bigness sweeps my being like a flood.
Yet as a rebel fronts a king in state,
I stand within her walls with not a shred
Of terror, malice, not a word of jeer.
Darkly I gaze into the days ahead,
And see her might and granite wonders there,
Beneath the touch of Time's unerring hand,
Like priceless treasures sinking in the sand.

The Lynching

His Spirit in smoke ascended to high heaven.
His father, by the cruelest way of pain,
Had bidden him to his bosom once again;
The awful sin remained still unforgiven.
All night a bright and solitary star
(Perchance the one that ever guided him,
Yet gave him up at last to Fate's wild whim)
Hung pitifully o'er the swinging char.
Day dawned, and soon the mixed crowds came to view
The ghastly body swaying in the sun
The women thronged to look, but never a one
Showed sorrow in her eyes of steely blue;
And little lads, lynchers that were to be,
Danced round the dreadful thing in fiendish glee.

If We Must Die

If we must die, let it not be like hogs
Hunted and penned in an inglorious spot,
While round us bark the mad and hungry dogs,
Making their mock at our accursèd lot.
If we must die, O let us nobly die,
So that our precious blood may not be shed
In vain; then even the monsters we defy
Shall be constrained to honor us though dead!
O kinsmen! we must meet the common foe!
Though far outnumbered let us show us brave,
And for their thousand blows deal one deathblow!
What though before us lies the open grave?
Like men we'll face the murderous, cowardly pack,
Pressed to the wall, dying, but fighting back!

Flame-Heart

So much have I forgotton in ten years,
    So much in ten brief years!   I have forgot
What time the purple apples come to juice,
    And what month brings the shy forget-me-not.
I have forgot the special, startling season
    Of the pimento's flowering and fruiting;
What time of year the ground doves brown the fields
    And fill the noonday with their curious fluting.
I have forgotten much, but still remember
The poinsettia's red, blood-red in warm December.

I still recall the honey-fever grass,
    But cannot recollect the high days when
We rooted them out of the ping-wing path
    To stop the mad bees in the rabbit pen.
I often try to think in what sweet month
    The languid painted ladies used to dapple
The yellow by-road mazing from the main,
    Sweet with the golden threads of the rose-apple.
I have forgotten — strange — but quite remember
The poinsettia's red, blood-red in warm December.

The Harlem Dancer

Applauding youths laughed with young prostitutes
And watched her perfect, half-clothed body sway;
Her voice was like the sound of blended flutes
Blown by black players upon a picnic day.
She sang and danced on gracefully and calm,
The light gauze hanging loose about her form;
To me she seemed a proudly-swaying palm
Grown lovelier for passing through a storm.
Upon her swarthy neck black shiny curls
Luxuriant fell; and tossing coins in praise,
The wine-flushed, bold-eyed boys, and even the girls,
Devoured her shape with eager, passionate gaze;
But looking at her falsely-smiling face,
I knew her self was not in that strange place.

Flower of Love

The perfume of your body dulls my sense.
    I want nor wine nor weed; your breath alone
Suffices.   In this moment rare and tense
    I worship at your breast.   The flower is blown,
The saffron petals tempt my amorous mouth,
    The yellow heart is radiant now with dew
Soft-scented, redolent of my loved South;
    O flower of love! I give myself to you.
Uncovered on your couch of figured green,
    Here let us linger indivisible.
The portals of your sanctuary unseen
    Receive my offering, yielding unto me.
Oh, with our love the night is warm and deep!
    The air is sweet, my flower, and sweet the flute
Whose music lulls our burning brain to sleep,
    While we lie loving, passionate and mute.

Jean Toomer (1894-1967)

In 1923 Jean Toomer seemed destined to be a major American writer. His poems and stories were eagerly sought by editors, and he had received accolades from such writers and critics as Sherwood Anderson, Waldo Frank, Gorham Munson, and W. S. Braithwaite. Except for a privately printed collection of aphorisms, however, Jean Toomer published no books after 1923. He remains, therefore, an important but tragic figure in black American literature.

Born in Washington, D. C., Nathan Eugene Toomer was the grandson of P. B. S. Pinchback, who, during Reconstruction, served briefly as Acting Governor of Louisiana. After enrolling briefly at the University of Wisconsin, the American College of Physical Training, the University of Chicago, the City College of New York, and New York University, where he considered and rejected studies in agriculture, physical education, medicine, sociology, and history, Jean Toomer settled on a career as a writer. Following an apprenticeship as a writer in New York City and Washington, he accepted a position as acting principal in Sparta, Georgia, in the fall of 1922. Inspired with the belief that he had located his roots in the ancestral home of his people, Toomer wrote poems, stories, and sketches, especially about Southern women whose quests for identity brought them into conflict with the prevalent moral attitudes of American society. When he returned to Washington, he added stories, poems, and sketches about the more inhibited black people of Washington and Chicago. He collected and published all of these as *Cane* (1923), a classic in black American literature.

Toomer's personal search for identity, however, did not end with *Cane*. A student of Eastern philosophies, he found a spiritual leader in George Gurdjieff and dedicated himself to teaching the Gurdjieffan ideas to the American people. Thus, he smothered his lyricism under a shroud of satire and didacticism as he substituted psychological case studies for sympathetic sketches. When publishers rejected these works, he accused them of restricting him to

53

Negro subjects. Searching for freedom to develop, he argued that he should be judged as an American rather than a Negro; subsequently, he denied that he had any Negro ancestors. Americans refused to accept his racial stance. A national magazine made national scandal of his marriage to Caucasian Margery Latimer, a promising writer who had been his disciple in a Gurdjieffan experiment, which the newspapers characterized as a "free love" colony. Toomer attempted to answer his critics by writing novels about his marriage and about the Gurdjieffan philosophy. Publishers continued to reject them. He also wrote essays in which he explained the philosophy and his belief that America would give birth to a new race — neither white nor black but American.

The tragic death of his wife in childbirth, the Depression, and rejections by publishers made the Thirties a decade of tragedy relieved only by a second marriage. For the remainder of his life, Toomer searched for spiritual understanding through the Society of Friends, psychiatry, and Indian mysticism. Occasionally he lectured to college students and to gatherings of the Friends. He continued to write plays, novels, poems, and stories; but, except for an occasional poem or sketches, his efforts went unpublished. He died in a rest home in 1967.

Jean Toomer's best writing is a lyric impressionism which suggests poetry even when he used the medium of prose. Speaking from this point of view, one can say that Toomer's actual verse, consequently, represents only a small sampling of his poetry.

The following four selections represent his later writing. *The Blue Meridian*, Toomer's longest poem, presents his social philosophy that the intermingling of various races on this continent has produced a new race. *The Blue Meridian* was never published in entirety; only the first eighty-eight lines have been published previously, as "Brown River, Smile." In the lines selected here Toomer concludes his tribute to the individual races and to the new world which their fusion will create. All four of the following selections are published for the first time.

from The Blue Meridian

Each new American
The old gods, led by an inverted Christ,
A shaved Moses, a blanched Lemur,
And a moulting dollar,

Withdrew into the distance and soon died,
Their dust and seed falling down
To fertilize the five regions of America.

We are waiting for a new God.

The old peoples —
The great European races sent wave after wave
That washed the forests, the earth's rich loam,
Grew towns with the seeds of giant cities,
Made roads, laid golden rails,
Factoried superb machines,
Sang once of the swift achievement,
And died because it ceased to feel.

    Late minstrels of the restless earth,
    No muteness can be granted thee,
    Lift thy laughing energies
    To that white point which is a star.

The great African races sent a single wave
And singing riplets to sorrow in red fields,
Sing a swan song, to break rocks
And immortalize a hiding water boy.

    I'm leaving the shining ground, brothers,
    I sing because I ache,
    I go because I must,
    Brothers, I am leaving the shining ground;
    Don't ask me where,
    I'll meet you there,
    I'm leaving the shining ground.

The great red race was here.
In a land of flaming earth and torrent-rains,
Of red sea-plains and majestic mesas,
At sunset from a purple hill
The Gods came down;
They serpentined into pueblo,
And a white-robed priest
Danced with them five days and nights;
But pueblo, priest, and Shalikoo

Sank into the sacred earth
To fertilize the five regions of America.

Hi-ye, hi-yo, hi-yo,
Hi-ye, hi-yo, hi-yo,
A lone eagle feather,
An untamed Navajo,
The ghosts of buffaloes,
Hi-ye, hi-yo, hi-yo,
Hi-ye, hi-yo, hi-yo.

We who exist today are the new people,
Born of elevated rock and lifted branches,
A race called the Americans;
And we are the old people; we are witnesses
That behind us there extends
An unbroken chain of ancestors;
Of millions of fathers through a million years
We are the breathing receptacles.
Mankind is a cross —
The solid stream sourcing in the remote past,
Ending in far off distant years,
Is the perpendicular;
The planetary wash of those new living
Forms the transverse bar. . . .

O thou, Relentless Stream, . . .
The Mississippi, sister of the Ganges,
Main artery of earth in the western world,
Is waiting to become
In the spirit of America, a sacred river.
Whoever lifts the Mississippi
Lifts himself and all America;
Whoever lifts himself
Makes that great brown river smile.
The blood of earth and the blood of man
Course swifter and rejoice when we spiritualize.

The east coast is masculine,
The west coast is feminine,
The middle region is the child —
Force of reconciling

And generator of symbols,
Source of a new force —
It not another it will be Al Capone.

So split spirit can divide,
No dead soul can undermine thee,
Thou, great coasts and harbors,
Mountains, lakes, and plains,
Thou art the majestic base
Of cathedral people,
The seed which started thee has grown.

The prairie's sweep is flat infinity,
The city's rise is perpendicular to farthest star,
I stand where the two directions intersect,
At Michigan Avenue and Walton Place,
Parallel to my countrymen,
Right-angled to the universe.

Blue Meridian, banded-light,
Dynamic atom-aggregate,
Awoke and danced upon the earth;
In his left hand he held elevated rock,
In his right hand he held lifted branches,
He danced the dance of the Blue Meridian
And dervished with the five regions of America.

Lift, lift, thou waking forces!
Let us feel the energy of animals,
The energy of rumps and bull-bent heads
Crashing the barrier to man.
It must spiral on!
A million million men, or twelve men,
Must crash the barrier to the next higher form.

Beyond plants are animals,
Beyond animals is man,
Beyond man is God.

The Big Light,
Let the Big Light in!

O thou, Radiant Incorporeal,
The I of earth and of mankind, hurl
Down these seaboards, across this continent,
The thousand-rayed discus of thy mind,
And, above our walking limbs unfurl
Spirit-torsos of exquisite strength!

Five Vignettes

1

The red-tiled ships you see reflected,
Are nervous,
And afraid of clouds.

2

There, on the clothes-line
Still as she pinned them,
Pieces now the wind may wear.

3

The old man, at ninety,
Eating peaches,
Is he not afraid of worms?

4

Wear my thimble of agony
And when you sew,
No needle points will prick you.

5

In Y. Don's laundry
A Chinese baby fell
And cried as any other.

The Lost Dancer

Spatial depths of being survive
The birth to death recurrences

Of feet dancing on earth of sand;
Vibrations of the dance survive
The sand; the sand, elect, survives
The dancer. He can find no source
Of magic adequate to bind
The sand upon his feet, his feet
Upon his dance, his dance upon
The diamond body of his being.

At Sea

Once I saw large waves
Crested with white-caps;
A driving wind
Transformed the caps
Into scudding spray —
"Swift souls," I addressed them —
They turned towards me
Startled
Sea-descending faces;
But I, not they,
Felt the pang of transience.

Countee Cullen (1903-1946)

A native of New York City, Countee Cullen was popularly acclaimed the "poet laureate" of the Harlem Renaissance. He published his first collection of poems — *Color* (1925) — while still a student at New York University. Within the next two years, he earned a master's degree in English from Harvard, published two additional volumes of poetry — *The Ballad of the Brown Girl* (1927) and *Copper Sun* (1927), edited an anthology of poetry (1927), and wrote literary columns for *Opportunity* magazine. A Guggenheim fellowship enabled him to spend several months in France, where he completed *The Black Christ and Other Poems* (1929). Although his productivity slowed during his years as a high school teacher, he produced two additional volumes of poetry, one novel (*One Way to Heaven*, 1932), and two books for children.

Even though Cullen's early work earned praise for his use of Afro-American themes, his stylistic models were John Keats and A. E. Housman, and his poems sang of love and roses as often as of the Afro-American spirit. As he matured, Cullen frequently complained about critics' efforts to restrict him to subjects related to the Afro-American experience. Increasingly, he lamented the disillusionment of lost love and the sorrows of world's outcasts. When he abstained from Afro-American themes, however, his smooth, pure melodies on conventional subjects proved insufficient to distinguish him in a generation expecting vivid imagery and marked originality in poetry.

The following selections illustrate characteristic themes: affirmation of African heritage, the sorrow of love, and sympathy for the rejected.

Heritage
(*For Harold Jackman*)

What is Africa to me:
Copper sun or scarlet sea,
Jungle star or jungle track,
Strong bronzed men, or regal black
Women from whose loins I sprang
When the birds of Eden sang?
One three centuries removed
From the scenes his fathers loved,
Spicy grove, cinnamon tree,
What is Africa to me?

So I lie, who all day long
Want no sound except the song
Sung by wild barbaric birds
Goading massive jungle herds,
Juggernauts of flesh that pass
Trampling tall defiant grass
Where young forest lovers lie,
Plighting troth beneath the sky.
So I lie, who always hear,
Though I cram against my ear
Both my thumbs, and keep them there,
Great drums throbbing through the air.
So I lie, whose fount of pride,
Dear distress, and joy allied,
Is my somber flesh and skin,
With the dark blood dammed within
Like great pulsing tides of wine
That, I fear, must burst the fine
Channels of the chafing net
Where they surge and foam and fret.

Africa? A book one thumbs
Listlessly, till slumber comes.
Unremembered are her bats
Circling through the night, her cats
Crouching in the river reeds,
Stalking gentle flesh that feeds
By the river brink; no more

Does the bugle-throated roar
Cry that monarch claws have leapt
From the scabbards where they slept.
Silver snakes that once a year
Doff the lovely coats you wear,
Seek no covert in your fear
Lest a mortal eye should see;
What's your nakedness to me?
Here no leprous flowers rear
Fierce corollas in the air;
Here no bodies sleek and wet,
Dripping mingled rain and sweat,
Tread the savage measures of
Jungle boys and girls in love.
What is last year's snow to me,
Last year's anything? The tree
Budding yearly must forget
How its past arose or set —
Bough and blossom, flower, fruit,
Even what shy bird with mute
Wonder at her travail there,
Meekly labored in its hair.
One three centuries removed
From the scenes his fathers loved,
Spicy grove, cinnamon tree,
What is Africa to me?

So I lie, who find no peace
Night or day, no slight release
From the unremittant beat
Made by cruel padded feet
Walking through my body's street.
Up and down they go, and back,
Treading out a jungle track.
So I lie, who never quite
Safely sleep from rain at night —
I can never rest at all
When the rain begins to fall;
Like a soul gone mad with pain
I must match its weird refrain;
Ever must I twist and squirm,

Writhing like a baited worm,
While its primal measures drip
Through my body, crying, "Strip!
Doff this new exuberance.
Come and dance the Lover's Dance!"
In an old remembered way
Rain works on me night and day.

Quaint, outlandish heathen gods
Black men fashion out of rods,
Clay, and brittle bits of stone,
In a likeness like their own,
My conversion came high-priced;
I belong to Jesus Christ,
Preacher of humility;
Heathen gods are naught to me.

Father, Son, and Holy Ghost,
So I make an idle boast;
Jesus of the twice-turned cheek,
Lamb of God, although I speak
With my mouth thus, in my heart
Do I play a double part.
Ever at Thy glowing altar
Must my heart grow sick and falter,
Wishing He I served were black,
Thinking then it would not lack
Precedent of pain to guide it,
Let who would or might deride it;
Surely then this flesh would know
Yours had borne a kindred woe.
Lord, I fashion dark gods, too,
Daring even to give You
Dark despairing features where,
Crowned with dark rebellious hair,
Patience wavers just so much as
Mortal grief compels, while touches
Quick and hot, of anger, rise
To smitten cheek and weary eyes.
Lord, forgive me if my need
Sometimes shapes a human creed.
All day long and all night through,

One thing only must I do:
Quench my pride and cool my blood,
Lest I perish in the flood.
Lest a hidden ember set
Timber that I thought was wet
Burning like the dryest flax,
Melting like the merest wax,
Lest the grave restore its dead.
Not yet has my heart or head
In the least way realized
They and I are civilized.

From the Dark Tower
(To Charles S. Johnson)

We shall not always plant while others reap
The golden increment of bursting fruit,
Not always countenance, abject and mute,
That lesser men should hold their brothers cheap;
Not everlastingly while others sleep
Shall we beguile their limbs with mellow flute,
Not always bend to some more subtle brute;
We were not made eternally to weep.

The night whose sable breast relieves the stark,
White stars is no less lovely being dark,
And there are buds that cannot bloom at all
In light, but crumple, piteous, and fall;
So in the dark we hide the heart that bleeds,
And wait, and tend our agonizing seeds.

Song in Spite of Myself

Never love with all your heart,
    It only ends in aching;
And bit by bit to the smallest part
    That organ will be breaking.

Never love with all your mind,
    It only ends in fretting;

In musing on sweet joys behind,
    Too poignant for forgetting.

Never love with all your soul,
    For such there is no ending,
Though a mind that frets may find control,
    And a shattered heart find mending.

Give but a grain of the heart's rich seed,
    Confine some under cover,
And when love goes, bid him God-speed.
    And find another lover.

Magnets

The straight, the swift, the debonair,
Are targets on the thoroughfare
For every kind appraising eye;
Sweet words are said as they pass by.
But such a strange contrary thing
My heart is, it will never cling
To any bright unblemished thing.
Such have their own security,
And little need to lean on me.
The limb that falters in its course,
And cries, "Not yet!" to waning force;
The orb that may not brave the sun;
The bitter mouth, its kissing done;
The loving heart that must deny
The very love it travels by;
What most has need to bend and pray,
These magnets draw my heart their way.

For Paul Laurence Dunbar

Born of the sorrowful of heart,
    Mirth was a crown upon his head;
Pride kept his twisted lips apart
    In jest, to hide a heart that bled.

Langston Hughes (1902-1967)

Langston Hughes has been described as the most versatile Afro-American writer who ever lived. Born in Joplin, Missouri, reared in Kansas and Ohio, he entered Columbia University in 1922 but dropped out after a year of studying. For several years, he worked his way through Europe and Africa before returning to America, where he soon became a part of the Harlem Renaissance. After completing undergraduate study at Lincoln University (Pa.), Hughes became a professional writer and lecturer.

No other Negro writer has matched the variety of Hughes' achievements. Among his more than thirty books are nine volumes of poems, two novels, and three collections of stories. Fascinated by theater, he established several all-Negro theatrical companies. Three of his plays were produced on Broadway, and one — *Mulatto* (1934) — enjoyed the longest continuous run of any play written by a Negro before Lorraine Hansberry. In addition, Hughes wrote the libretto for the musical version of Elmer Rice's *Street Scene*, an opera, stories for children, and two autobiographies. He also translated poetry, edited or co-edited anthologies of folklore and poetry, and publicized the musical and literary achievements of Africans and Afro-Americans. Perhaps his most significant literary achievement lies in the many stories, sketches, and essays about Jesse B. Semple ("Simple").

Although he developed all of the conventional themes in poetry, Langston Hughes most often concerned himself with the Afro-American as subject. Forty years before the present generation's proclamation that "Black is beautiful," Langston Hughes was emphasizing the theme, encouraging black people to be proud of their identity, evoking sympathy for victims of racial discrimination, promoting closer relationships among all classes of black people, ridiculing the assininities of bigotry, revealing the mixtures of gaiety and melancholy in the Harlem he loved, and celebrating the

67

common man. Because he continued to write for more than forty
years, Hughes, better than any other writer of the Harlem Renais-
sance, kept alive the gaiety and exuberance of that period; but he
also revealed the underlying sorrow for which laughter was both a
scab and a shield.

From his earliest poetry to the last, Hughes sought to reproduce
the rhythms characteristic of the Afro-American music. In the
Twenties and the Thirties, he became known for his "blues" and
his imitations of jazz rhythms. As musical styles changed, Hughes
experimented with boogie-woogie and be-bop. Frequently, in his
later years, he read to the accompaniment of jazz, and a recent
book of poems, *Ask Your Mama*, provides notes for musical effects
to underscore the reading.

The first two of the following selections illustrate the rhythms
and racial pride of Hughes' early poetry. "The Weary Blues," a
sympathetic portrait, reveals in the song of musician the character-
istic style of Hughes' blues poetry — a long line; the line repeated,
possibly with variation; and a third line rhyming with the first two.
In the next selections, written twenty-five years later than the first,
new rhythms support the familiar themes.

The final selection presents one incident in the life of Madam
Alberta K. Johnson, a soul sister of Jesse B. Semple.

Dream Variation

To fling my arms wide
In some place of the sun,
To whirl and to dance
Till the white day is done.
Then rest at cool evening
Beneath a tall tree
While night comes on gently,
    Dark like me, —
That is my dream!

To fling my arms wide
In the face of the sun,
Dance! whirl! whirl!
Till the quick day is done.
Rest at pale evening. . . .
A tall, slim tree. . . .

Night coming tenderly
Black like me.

Epilogue

I, too, sing America.

I am the darker brother.
They send me to eat in the kitchen
When company comes,
But I laugh,
And eat well,
And grow strong.

Tomorrow,
I'll sit at the table
When company comes.
Nobody'll dare
Say to me,
"Eat in the kitchen,"
Then.

Besides,
They'll see how beautiful I am
And be ashamed, —

I, too, am America.

The Weary Blues

Droning a drowsy syncopated tune,
Rocking back and forth to a mellow croon,
    I heard a Negro play.
Down on Lenox Avenue the other night
By the pale dull pallor of an old gas light
    He did a lazy sway. . . .
    He did a lazy sway. . . .
To the tune o' those Weary Blues.
With his ebony hands on each ivory key
He made that poor piano moan with melody.
    O Blues!

Swaying to and fro on his rickety stool
He played that sad raggy tune like a musical fool.
　Sweet Blues!
Coming from a black man's soul.
　O Blues!
In a deep song voice with a melancholy tone
I heard that Negro sing, that old piano moan —
　"Ain't got nobody in all this world,
　Ain't got nobody but ma self.
　I's gwine to quit ma frownin'
　And put ma troubles on the shelf."
Thump, thump, thump, went his foot on the floor.
He played a few chords then he sang some more —
　"I got the Weary Blues
　And I can't be satisfied.
　Got the Weary Blues
　And can't be satisfied —
　I ain't happy no mo'
　And I wish that I had died."
And far into the night he crooned that tune.
The stars went out and so did the moon.
The singer stopped playing and went to bed
While the Weary Blues echoed through his head.
He slept like a rock or a man that's dead.

Theme For English B

The instructor said,

Go home and write
a page tonight.
And let that page come out of you ——
Then, it will be true.

I wonder if it's that simple?

I am twenty-two, colored, born in Winston-Salem.
I went to school there, then Durham, then here
to this college on the hill above Harlem.
I am the only colored student in my class.
The steps from the hill lead down into Harlem,
through a park, then I cross St. Nicholas,

Eighth Avenue, Seventh, and I come to the Y,
the Harlem Branch Y, where I take the elevator
up to my room, sit down, and write this page:

It's not easy to know what is true for you or me
at twenty-two, my age. But I guess I'm what
I feel and see and hear. Harlem, I hear you:
hear you, hear me — we two — you, me, talk on this page.
(I hear New York, too.) Me — who?

Well, I like to eat, sleep, drink, and be in love.
I like to work, read, learn, and understand life.
I like a pipe for a Christmas present,
or records — Bessie, bop, or Bach.
I guess being colored doesn't make me *not* like
the same things other folks like who are other races.
So will my page be colored that I write?
Being me, it will not be white.
But it will be
a part of you, instructor.
You are white ——
yet a part of me, as I am a part of you.
That's American.
Sometimes perhaps you don't want to be a part of me.
Nor do I often want to be a part of you.
But we are, that's true!
As I learn from you,
I guess you learn from me ——
although you're older — and white ——
and somewhat more free.

This is my page for English B.

College Formal: Renaissance Casino

Golden girl
in a golden gown
in a melody night
in Harlem town
lad tall and brown
tall and wise
college boy smart

eyes in eyes
the music wraps
them both around
in mellow magic
of dancing sound
till they're the heart
of the whole big town
gold and brown

Madam and Her Madam

I worked for a woman,
She wasn't mean —
But she had a twelve-room
House to clean.

Had to get breakfast,
Dinner, and supper, too —
Then take care of her children
When I got through.

Wash, iron, and scrub,
Walk the dog around —
It was too much,
Nearly broke me down.

I said, Madam,
Can it be
You trying to make a
Pack-horse out of me?

She opened her mouth.
She cried, Oh, no!
You know, Alberta,
I love you so!

I said, Madam,
That may be true —
But I'll be dogged
If I love you!

Arna Bontemps (1902-   )

Novelist, poet, editor, historian, biographer, librarian, teacher, Arna Bontemps, like his friend Langston Hughes, has distinguished himself in a variety of literary fields. Born in Louisiana, but reared in California, where he graduated from Pacific Union College in 1923, Bontemps, who studied further at Columbia and the University of Chicago, was librarian at Fisk University from 1943 to 1966. Since then he has taught at the University of Illinois at Chicago Circle and at Yale University.

One of the bright young writers who migrated to Harlem during the Renaissance, Bontemps achieved his first significant publication as a novelist — *God Sends Sunday* (1932); *Black Thunder* (1936), a history of the slave Gabriel's abortive rebellion in Virginia in 1800; and *Drums at Dusk* (1939), the story of the successful revolution of Haitian slaves. Dissatisfied with the literature available for his children and other Afro-American children, Bontemps wrote juvenile literature (biography, fiction, poetry, and history), more in fact than any other Negro author, and has received the Jane Addams Children's Book Award. Recipient of Guggenheim and Rosenwald fellowships and of various other awards for writing, Bontemps has edited poetry and co-edited folklore. His best-known works of non-fiction for adults are *Any Place But Here* (1966), originally entitled *They Seek a City* and written in collaboration with Jack Conroy, and *100 Years of Negro Freedom* (1961).

Although his collection of poetry was not published until 1963, the poems were written during the Harlem Renaissance.

Southern Mansion

Poplars are standing there still as death
and ghosts of dead men

73

meet their ladies walking
two by two beneath the shade
and standing on the marble steps.

There is a sound of music echoing
through the open door
and in the field there is
another sound tinkling in the cotton:
chains of bondmen dragging on the ground.

The years go back with an iron clank,
a hand is on the gate,
a dry leaf trembles on the wall.
Ghosts are walking.
They have broken roses down
and poplars stand there still as death.

Nocturne at Bethesda

I thought I saw an angel flying low.
I thought I saw the flicker of a wing
above the mulberry trees — but not again.
Bethesda sleeps. This ancient pool that healed
a host of bearded Jews does not awake.
This pool that once the angels troubled does not move.
No angel stirs it now, no Saviour comes
with healing in His hands to raise the sick
and bid the lame man leap upon the ground.

The golden days are gone. Why do we wait
so long upon the marble steps, blood
falling from our open wounds? And why
do our black faces search the empty sky?
Is there something we have forgotten? some precious thing
we have lost, wandering in strange lands?

There was a day, I remember now,
I beat my breast and cried 'Wash me God,
wash me with a wave of wind upon
the barley; O quiet One, draw near, draw near!

walk upon the hills with lovely feet
and in the waterfall stand and speak.

Dip white hands in the lily pool and mourn
upon the harps still hanging in the trees
near Babylon along the river's edge,
but oh, remember me, I pray, before
the summer goes and rose leaves lose their red.'

The old terror takes my heart, the fear
of quiet waters and of faint twilights.
There will be better days when I am gone
and healing pools where I cannot be healed.
Fragrant stars will gleam forever and ever
above the place where I lie desolate.

Yet I hope, still I long to live.
And if there can be returning after death
I shall come back. But it will not be here:
if you want me you must search for me
beneath the palms of Africa. Or if
I am not there then you may call to me
across the shining dunes, perhaps I shall
be following a desert caravan.

I may pass through centuries of death
with quiet eyes, but I'll remember still
a jungle tree with burning scarlet birds.
There is something I have forgotten, some precious thing.
I shall be seeking ornaments of ivory,
I shall be dying for a jungle fruit.

You do not hear, Bethesda.
O still green water in a stagnant pool!
Love abandoned you and me alike.
There was a day you held a rich full moon
upon your heart and listened to the words
of men now dead and saw the angels fly.
There is a simple story on your face:
years have wrinkled you. I know, Bethesda!
You are sad. It is the same with me.

Sterling Brown (1901-   )

Born in Washington, D. C., Sterling Brown is a major authority on the Negro as writer and as character in American literature. Educated at Williams College and at Harvard University, where he received a Master of Arts degree, Brown has written extensively on the literature, language, drama, poetry, and music of Afro-Americans. His best-known book-length studies are *The Negro in American Fiction* (1937) and *Negro Poetry and Drama* (1937). He also served as senior editor of *The Negro Caravan* (1941), the most comprehensive anthology prior to the present decade.

Brown earned his early literary reputation, however, for satiric and lyric poetry on racial themes. Zestfully he satirized white-black relationships in the South; but, with the spirit of the Harlem Renaissance, he also realistically revealed the foibles of black people.

Slim Greer

Listen to the tale
Of Ole Slim Greer,
Waitines' devil
Waitin' here;

Talkinges' guy
An' biggest liar,
With always a new lie
On the fire.

Tells a tale
Of Arkansaw
That keeps the kitchen
In a roar;

Tells in a long-drawled
Careless tone,
As solemn as a Baptist
Parson's moan.

How he in Arkansaw
Passed for white,
An' he no lighter
Than a dark midnight.

Found a nice white woman
At a dance,
Thought he was from Spain
Or else from France;

Nobody suspicioned
Ole Slim Greer's race
But a Hill Billy, always
Roun' the place,

Who called one day
On the trustful dame
An' found Slim comfy
When he came.

The whites lef' the parlor
All to Slim
Which didn't cut
No ice with him,

An' he started a-tinklin'
Some mo'nful blues,
An' a-pattin' the time
With No. Fourteen shoes.

The cracker listened
An' then he spat
An' said, "No white man
Could play like that. . . ."

The white jane ordered
The tattler out;

Then, female-like,
Began to doubt,

Crept into the parlor
Soft as you please,
Where Slim was agitatin'
The ivories.

Heard Slim's music —
An' then, hot damn!
Shouted sharp — "Nigger!"
An' Slim said, "Ma'am?"

She screamed and the crackers
Swarmed up soon,
But found only echoes
Of his tune;

'Cause Slim had sold out
With lightnin' speed;
"Hope I may die, sir —
Yes, indeed. . . ."

Long Gone

I laks yo' kin' of lovin',
    Ain't never caught you wrong,
But it jes' ain' nachal
    Fo' to stay here long;

It jes' ain' nachal
    Fo' a railroad man,
With a itch fo' travelin'
    He cain't understan'. . . .

I looks at de rails,
    An' I looks at de ties,
An' I hears an ole freight
    Puffin' up de rise,

An' at nights on my pallet,
    When all is still,
I listens fo' de empties
    Bumpin' up de hill;

When I oughta be quiet,
    I is got a itch
Fo' to hear de whistle blow
    Fo' de crossin' or de switch,

An' I knows de time's a-nearin'
    When I got to ride,
Though it's homelike and happy
    At yo' side.

You is done all you could do
    To make me stay;
'Tain't no fault of yours I'se leavin' —
    I'se jes dataway.

I don't know which way I'm travelin' —
    Far or near,
All I knows fo' certain is
    I cain't stay here.

Ain't no call at all, sweet woman,
    Fo' to carry on —
Jes' my name and jes' my habit
    To be Long Gone. . . .

Return

I have gone back in boyish wonderment
To things that I had foolishly put by. . . .
Have found an alien and unknown content
In seeing how some bits of cloud-filled sky
Are framed in bracken pools; through chuckling hours
Have watched the antic frogs, or curiously
Have numbered all the unnamed, vagrant flowers,
That fleck the unkempt meadows, lavishly.

Or where a headlong toppling stream has stayed
Its racing, lulled to quiet by the song
Bursting from out the thick-leaved oaken shade,
There I have lain while hours sauntered past —
I have found peacefulness somewhere at last,
Have found a quiet needed for so long.

Southern Road

Swing dat hammer — hunh —
Steady, bo';
Swing dat hammer — hunh —
Steady, bo';
Ain't no rush, bebby,
Long ways to go.

Burner tore his — hunh —
Black heart away;
Burner tore his — hunh —
Black heart away;
Got me life, bebby,
An' a day.

Gal's on Fifth Street — hunh —
Son done gone;
Gal's on Fifth Street — hunh —
Son done gone;
Wife's in de ward, bebby,
Babe's not bo'n.

My ole man died — hunh —
Cussin' me;
My ole man died — hunh —
Cussin' me;
Ole lady rocks, bebby,
Huh misery.

Doubleshackled — hunh —
Guard behin';
Doubleshackled — hunh —

Guard behin';
Ball an' chain, bebby,
On my min'.

White man tells me — hunh —
Damn yo' soul;
White man tells me — hunh —
Damn yo' soul;
Got no need, bebby,
To be tole.

Chain gang nevah -— hunh —
Let me go;
Chain gang nevah — hunh —
Let me go;
Po' los' boy, bebby,
Evahmo'. . . .

Melvin B. Tolson (1900-1966)

Melvin B. Tolson elicited accolades from critics and poets. Upon reading a section of Tolson's *Libretto for the Republic of Liberia* (1953), Allen Tate declared, "For the first time . . . a Negro poet has assimilated completely the full poetic language of his time and, by implication, the language of the Anglo-American poetic tradition." With even more enthusiasm though contrasting evaluation, Karl Shapiro, in the introduction to Tolson's final book, *Harlem Gallery* (1965), described Tolson as a poet who "writes and thinks in Negro" and, thus, would expand the poetic language. Despite similar approbation by such poets as John Ciardi, Langston Hughes, and Robert Frost, M. B. Tolson's general recognition as a poet has been limited.

Born in Moberly, Missouri, he was educated at Fisk University, Lincoln University in Pennsylvania (B.A.), and Columbia University (M.A.). For many years, he taught English, coached debating, and directed drama at Wiley College and Langston University, where he developed extraordinary popularity among students. His ability to charm voters enabled him to win election four times to the position of mayor of Langston, Oklahoma.

Although Tolson also wrote drama, he achieved his excellence in poetry. In 1944 he published his first volume of verse, *Rendezvous with America*. In 1947, he was commissioned poet laureate of Liberia to compose a poem, which was published in 1953—*Libretto for the Republic of Liberia*. His last book was *The Harlem Gallery: Book I, The Curator* (1965).

An admirer of Hart Crane and Ezra Pound, Tolson achieved increasing complexity in his use of language and allusion. Written in a style far simpler than that of his late work, "Dark Symphony" was his first poem to gain significant attention. It traces the history of the black man in America and concludes with a prophecy of triumph for the New Negro.

Dark Symphony

I

Allegro Moderato

Black Crispus Attucks taught
                Us how to die
Before white Patrick Henry's bugle breath
Uttered the vertical
                Transmitting cry:
"Yea, give me liberty or give me death."

Waifs of the auction block,
                Men black and strong
The juggernauts of despotism withstood,
Loin-girt with faith that worms
                Equate the wrong
And dust is purged to create brotherhood.

No Banquo's ghost can rise
                Against us now,
Aver we hobnailed Man beneath the brute,
Squeezed down the thorns of greed
                On Labor's brow,
Garroted lands and carted off the loot.

II

Lento Grave

The centuries-old pathos in our voices
Saddens the great white world,
And the wizardry of our dusky rhythms
Conjures up shadow-shapes of ante-bellum years:

Black slaves singing *One More River to Cross*
In the torture tombs of slave-ships,
Black slaves singing *Steal Away to Jesus*
In jungle swamps,
Black slaves singing *The Crucifixion*
In slave-pens at midnight,
Black slaves singing *Swing Low, Sweet Chariot*

In cabins of death,
Black slaves singing *Go Down, Moses*
In the canebrakes of the Southern Pharaohs.

III

Andante Sostenuto

They tell us to forget
The Golgotha we tread . . .
We who are scourged with hate,
A price upon our head.
They who have shackled us
Require of us a song,
They who have wasted us
Bid us condone the wrong.

They tell us to forget
Democracy is spurned.
They tell us to forget
The Bill of Rights is burned.
Three hundred years we slaved,
We slave and suffer yet:
Though flesh and bone rebel,
They tell us to forget!

Oh, how can we forget
Our human rights denied?
Oh, how can we forget
Our manhood crucified?
When Justice is profaned
And plea with curse is met,
When Freedom's gates are barred,
Oh, how can we forget?

IV

Tempo Primo

The New Negro strides upon the continent
In seven-league boots . . .
The New Negro
Who sprang from the vigor-stout loins

Of Nat Turner, gallows-martyr for Freedom,
Of Joseph Cinquez, Black Moses of the Amistad Mutiny,
Of Frederick Douglass, oracle of the Catholic Man,
Of Sojourner Truth, eye and ear of Lincoln's legions,
Of Harriet Tubman, Saint Bernard of the Underground Railroad.

The New Negro
Breaks the icons of his detractors,
Wipes out the conspiracy of silence,
Speaks to *his* America:
"My history-moulding ancestors
Planted the first crops of wheat on these shores,
Built ships to conquer the seven seas,
Erected the Cotton Empire,
Flung railroads across a hemisphere,
Disemboweled the earth's iron and coal,
Tunneled the mountains and bridged rivers,
Harvested the grain and hewed forests,
Sentineled the Thirteen Colonies,
Unfurled Old Glory at the North Pole,
Fought a hundred battles for the Republic."

The New Negro:
His giant hands fling murals upon high chambers,
His drama teaches a world to laugh and weep,
His music leads continents captive,
His voice thunders the Brotherhood of Labor,
His science creates seven wonders,
His Republic of Letters challenges the Negro-baiters.

The New Negro,
Hard-muscled, Fascist-hating, Democracy-ensouled,
Strides in seven-league boots
Along the Highway of Today
Toward the Promised Land of Tomorrow!

V

Larghetto

None in the Land can say
To us black men Today:

You send the tractors on their bloody path,
And create Okies for *The Grapes of Wrath.*
You breed the slum that breeds a *Native Son*
To damn the good earth Pilgrim Fathers won.

None in the Land can say
To us black men Today:
You dupe the poor with rags-to-riches tales,
And leave the workers empty dinner pails.
You stuff the ballot box, and honest men
Are muzzled by your demagogic din.

None in the Land can say
To us black men Today:
You smash stock markets with your coined blitzkriegs,
And make a hundred million guinea pigs.
You counterfeit our Christianity,
And bring contempt upon Democracy.

None in the Land can say
To us black men Today:
You prowl when citizens are fast asleep,
And hatch Fifth Column plots to blast the deep
Foundations of the State and leave the Land
A vast Sahara with a Fascist brand.

VI

Tempo di Marcia

Out of abysses of Illiteracy,
Through labyrinths of Lies,
Across waste lands of Disease . . .
We advance!

Out of dead-ends of Poverty,
Through wildernesses of Superstition,
Across barricades of Jim Crowism . . .
We advance!

With the Peoples of the World . . .
We advance!

Robert E. Hayden (1913-   )

At the World Festival of Negro Arts, held in Dakar, Senegal, in 1965, Robert Hayden won the Grand Prize for poetry, awarded for *A Ballad of Remembrance* (1962), his fourth volume of poetry. Born in Detroit, he attended Wayne State University and earned a Master's degree from the University of Michigan, where in 1938 and 1942, he received Avery Hopwood awards for poetry. A teacher at Fisk University from 1946 to 1968, he is presently on the faculty at the University of Michigan. In addition to *A Ballad of Remembrance*, he has published four volumes of poetry: *Heart-Shape in the Dust* (1940), *The Lion and the Archer* (with Myron O'Higgins, 1949), *Figure of Time* (1955), and *Selected Poems* (1966). He has also written drama and edited *Kaleidoscope: Poems by American Negro Poets* (1967).

An admirer of the verbal dexterities of William Butler Yeats, Hayden has provoked reaction from some recent black critics by insisting that a black poet should not be restricted to racial utterance. Despite the rhetoric of the debate, Robert Hayden, sensitively aware of his heritage, often has recreated incidents from the black man's history, paying eloquent tribute to Frederick Douglass, Nat Turner, Harriet Tubman, and the slaves who overthrew their jailors aboard the Spanish vessel, *The Amistad.*

In "Runagate, Runagate" he reproduces the yearning for liberty which motivated the slaves who followed the North Star and Harriet Tubman to freedom. The poem is a medley of voices: the narrator, the escaping slaves (their hopes expressed in spirituals), the slave masters advertising for their return, one slave who recalls Harriet Tubman, and the slave masters advertising a reward for her capture.

In "The Ballad of Nat Turner," Hayden focuses upon the vision which inspired Nat Turner to lead a slave rebellion in Virginia.

Runagate Runagate

I

Runs falls rises stumbles on from darkness into darkness
and the darkness thicketed with shapes of terror
and the hunters pursuing and the hounds pursuing
and the night cold and the night long and the river
to cross and the jack-muh-lanterns beckoning beckoning
and blackness ahead and when shall I reach that somewhere
morning and keep on going and never turn back and keep on going

>   Runagate
>   Runagate
>   Runagate

Many thousands rise and go
many thousands crossing over
>   O mythic North
>   O star-shaped yonder Bible city

Some go weeping and some rejoicing
some in coffins and some in carriages
some in silks and some in shackles

>   Rise and go or fare you well

No more auction block for me
no more driver's lash for me

>   If you see my Pompey, 30 yrs of age,
>   new breeches, plain stockings, negro shoes;
>   if you see my Anna, likely young mulatto
>   branded E on the right cheek, R on the left,
>   catch them if you can and notify subscriber.
>   Catch them if you can, but it won't be easy.
>   They'll dart underground when you try to catch them,
>   plunge into quicksand, whirlpools, mazes,
>   turn into scorpions when you try to catch them.

And before I'll be a slave
I'll be buried in my grave

North star and bonanza gold
I'm bound for the freedom, freedom-bound
and oh Susyanna don't you cry for me

Runagate

Runagate

II

Rises from their anguish and their power,

Harriet Tubman,

woman of earth, whipscarred,
a summoning, a shining

Mean to be free

And this was the way of it, brethren brethren,
way we journeyed from Can't to Can.
Moon so bright and no place to hide,
the cry up and the patterollers riding,
hound dogs belling in bladed air.
And fear starts a-murbling, Never make it,
we'll never make it. *Hush that now,*
and she's turned upon us, levelled pistol
glinting in the moonlight:
Dead folks can't jaybird-talk, she says;
you keep on going now or die, she says.

Wanted   Harriet Tubman   alias The General
alias Moses   Stealer of Slaves

In league with Garrison   Alcott   Emerson
Garrett   Douglass   Thoreau   John Brown

Armed and known to be Dangerous

Wanted   Reward   Dead or Alive

Tell me, Ezekiel, oh tell me do you see
mailed Jehovah coming to deliver me?

Hoot-owl calling in the ghosted air,
five times calling to the hants in the air.
Shadow of a face in the scary leaves,
shadow of a voice in the talking leaves:

Come ride-a my train

Oh that train, ghost-story train
through swamp and savanna movering movering,
over trestles of dew, through caves of the wish,
Midnight Special on a sabre track movering movering,
first stop Mercy and the last Hallelujah.

Come ride-a my train

Mean mean mean to be free.

The Ballad of Nat Turner

Then fled, O brethren, the wicked juba
    and wandered wandered far
from curfew joys in the Dismal's night.
    Fool of St. Elmo's fire

In scary night I wandered, praying,
    Lord God my harshener,
speak to me now or let me die;
    speak, Lord, to this mourner.

And came at length to livid trees
    where Ibo warriors
hung shadowless, turning in wind
    that moaned like Africa,

Their belltongue bodies dead, their eyes
    alive with the anger deep
in my own heart. Is this the sign,
    the sign forepromised me?

The spirits vanished. Afraid and lonely
    I wandered on in blackness.

Speak to me now or let me die.
　　Die, whispered the blackness.

And wild things gasped and scuffled in
　　the night; seething shapes
of evil frolicked upon the air.
　　I reeled with fear, I prayed.

Sudden brightness clove the preying
　　darkness, brightness that was
itself a golden darkness, brightness
　　so bright that it was darkness.

And there were angels, their faces hidden
　　from me, angels at war
with one another, angels in dazzling
　　combat. And oh the splendor,

The fearful splendor of that warring.
　　Hide me, I cried to rock and bramble.
Hide me, the rock, the bramble cried. . . .
　　How tell you of that holy battle?

The shock of wing on wing and sword
　　on sword was the tumult of
a taken city burning. I cannot
　　say how long they strove,

For the wheel in a turning wheel which is time
　　in eternity had ceased
its whirling, and owl and moccasin,
　　panther and nameless beast

And I were held like creatures fixed
　　in flaming, in fiery amber.
But I saw I saw oh many of
　　those mighty beings waver,

Waver and fall, go streaking down
　　into swamp water, and the water
hissed and steamed and bubbled and locked
　　shuddering shuddering over

The fallen and soon was motionless.
    Then that massive light
began a-folding slowly in
    upon itself, and I

Beheld the conqueror faces and, lo,
    they were like mine, I saw
they were like mine and in joy and terror
    wept, praising praising Jehovah.

Oh praised my honer, harshener
    till a sleep came over me,
a sleep heavy as death. And when
    I awoke at last free

And purified, I rose and prayed
    and returned after a time
to the blazing fields, to the humbleness.
    And bided my time.

Owen Dodson (1914-   )

A native of Brooklyn, New York, Owen Dodson was educated at Bates College and at Yale University, where he earned the Master of Fine Arts degree. A teacher at Spelman College and at Howard University, where he is currently head of the Drama Department, Owen Dodson has contributed significantly in Negro college theatre, a little-known but important training ground for black playwrights and performers. As a director, he has developed several of the black actors who are currently winning recognition in the professional theatre. Of the several plays he has written, the best-known is *Divine Comedy*, first produced at Yale University in 1938. Based on the story of Father Divine, it is probably the best verse drama written by a black playwright. His novel, *Boy at the Window* (1951), reprinted as *When Trees Were Green*, is distinguished by sensitive characterization and imaginative, sensuous description presented through the young protagonist. Both in his drama and in his fiction, Mr. Dodson has suggested rich poetic talent, revealed fully in his collection *Powerful Long Ladder* (1946). Taken from that volume, the following selections, written during World War II, consider the anguish of war and the hoped-for profits of peace.

For My Brother

VII

Sleep late with your dream.
The morning has a scar
To mark on the horizon
With the death of the morning star.

The color of blood will appear
And wash the morning sky,

Aluminum birds flying with fear
Will scream to your waking,
Will send you to die;

Sleep late with your dream.
Pretend that the morning is far,
Deep in the horizon country,
Unconcerned with the morning star.

Open Letter

Brothers, let us discover our hearts again,
Permitting the regular strong beat of humanity there
To propel the likelihood of other terror to an exit.

For at last it is nearly ended: the daily anguish needles
Probing in our brains when alarms crust the air
And planes stab over us.

(Tears screamed from our eyes,
Animals moaned for death, gardens were disguised,
Stumps strained to be whole again.)

For at last it is nearly ended, grass
Will be normal, hillsides
Pleased with boys roaming their bellies.

All the mourning children
Will understand the long word, hallelujah,
Each use for joy will light for them.

The torn souls and broken bodies will be restored,
Primers circulate for everlasting peace,
The doors to hope swung open.

Brothers, let us enter that portal for good
When peace surrounds us like a credible universe.
Bury that agony, bury this hate, take our black hands in yours.

Sorrow is the Only Faithful One

Sorrow is the only faithful one:
The lone companion clinging like a season
To its original skin no matter what the variations.

If all the mountains paraded
Eating the valleys as they went
And the sun were a coiffure on the highest peak,

Sorrow would be there between
The sparkling and the giant laughter
Of the enemy when the clouds come down to swim.

But I am less, unmagic, black,
Sorrow clings to me more than to doomsday mountains
Or erosion scars on a palisade.

Sorrow has a song like a leech
Crying because the sand's blood is dry
And the stars reflected in the lake

Are water for all their twinkling
And bloodless for all their charm.
I have blood, and a song.

Sorrow is the only faithful one.

Margaret Walker Alexander
(1915-   )

Born in Birmingham, Alabama, Margaret Walker received a B.A. from Northwestern University and completed her graduate study at the University of Iowa, where, instead of the usual theses, she submitted a collection of poems for the Master's degree and *Jubilee*, a historical novel about the Civil War period, for the doctorate. Both volumes have been published. A wife, a mother, a teacher of English at Livingstone College, West Virginia State College, and Jackson State College in Mississippi, a visiting professor at Northwestern University, and a recipient of a Rosenwald Fellowship, Margaret Walker Alexander is widely known for her volume of poetry, *For My People* (1942), which includes personal anguish, interest in Africa, racial pride, denunciations of the betrayers of black believers, and Negro folklore. The title poem of this volume is one of the most eloquent and understanding love poems ever addressed to black Americans.

For My People

For my people everywhere singing their slave songs repeatedly: their dirges and their ditties and their blues and jubilees, praying their prayers nightly to an unknown god, bending their knees humbly to an unseen power;

For my people lending their strength to the years, to the gone years and the now years and the maybe years, washing ironing cooking scrubbing sewing mending hoeing plowing digging planting pruning patching dragging along never gaining never reaping never knowing and never understanding;

For my playmates in the clay and dust and sand of Alabama
backyards playing baptizing and preaching and doc-
tor and jail and soldier and school and mama and
cooking and playhouse and concert and store and hair
and Miss Choomby and company;

For the cramped bewildered years we went to school to learn
to know the reasons why and the answers to and the
people who and the places where and the days when,
in memory of the bitter hours when we discovered we
were black and poor and small and different and
nobody cared and nobody wondered and nobody
understood;

For the boys and girls who grew in spite of these things to be
man and woman, to laugh and dance and sing and
play and drink their wine and religion and success, to
marry their playmates and bear children and then die
of consumption and anemia and lynching;

For my people thronging 47th Street in Chicago and Lenox
Avenue in New York and Rampart Street in New
Orleans, lost disinherited dispossessed and happy
people filling the cabarets and taverns and other
people's pockets needing bread and shoes and milk
and land and money and something — something all
our own;

For my people walking blindly spreading joy, losing time
being lazy, sleeping when hungry, shouting when
burdened, drinking when hopeless, tied and shackled
and tangled among ourselves by the unseen creatures
who tower over us omnisciently and laugh;

For my people blundering and groping and floundering in
the dark of churches and schools and clubs and
societies, associations and councils and committees
and conventions, distressed and disturbed and de-
ceived and devoured by money-hungry glory-craving
leeches, preyed on by facile force of state and fad and
novelty, by false prophet and holy believer;

For my people standing staring trying to fashion a better
way from confusion, from hypocrisy and misunder-
standing, trying to fashion a world that will hold all
the people, all the faces, all the adams and eves and
their countless generations;

Let a new earth rise. Let another world be born. Let a bloody
peace be written in the sky. Let a second generation
full of courage issue forth; let a people loving free-
dom come to growth. Let a beauty full of healing
and a strength of final clenching be the pulsing in
our spirits and our blood. Let the martial songs be
written, let the dirges disappear. Let a race of men
now rise and take control.

Gwendolyn Brooks (1917-   )

In 1950, Gwendolyn Brooks became the first Afro-American poet to receive a Pulitzer Prize for poetry (for *Annie Allen*, 1949). Born in Topeka, Kansas, she was reared in Chicago, where she completed her formal education at Wilson Junior College. For many years a housewife, she recently has accepted teaching positions at several colleges in Chicago and at the University of Wisconsin.

Her first volume of poetry, *A Street in Bronzeville*, was published in 1945. Subsequent volumes are *Bronzeville Boys and Girls* (poems for children, 1956), *The Bean Eaters* (1960), *Selected Poems* (1963), and *In the Mecca* (1968). In 1953, she published *Maud Martha*, a poetic novel about the maturing of a Negro girl.

Gwendolyn Brooks has earned praise both for technical artistry and for her sympathetic revelations of the Afro-American experience. A careful artist, she has experimented successfully with all of the traditional forms of short poetry, including the traditional ballad. Increasingly, in her later work, she has moved from relatively simple, suggestive, but grammatically complete, poetic statements to compressed phrases stripped of all words which can be spared. This development can be discerned from the stylistic differences between the first two of the following selections, taken from her first volume, and the last two, from her latest. As her style has changed, her thought has developed from emphasis upon the attitudes of a black *woman* to emphasis upon the ideas of black people in general.

Kitchenette Building

We are things of dry hours and the involuntary plan,
Grayed in, and gray. "Dream" makes a giddy sound, not strong
Like "rent," "feeding a wife," "satisfying a man."

But could a dream send up through onion fumes
Its white and violet, fight with fried potatoes
And yesterday's garbage ripening in the hall,
Flutter, or sing an aria down these rooms

Even if we were willing to let it in,
Had time to warm it, keep it very clean,
Anticipate a message, let it begin?

We wonder. But not well! not for a minute!
Since Number Five is out of the bathroom now,
We think of lukewarm water, hope to get in it.

The Womanhood

I. 2

What shall I give my children? who are poor,
Who are adjudged the leastwise of the land,
Who are my sweetest lepers, who demand
No velvet and no velvety velour;
But who have begged me for a brisk contour,
Crying that they are quasi, contraband
Because unfinished, graven by a hand
Less than angelic, admirable or sure.
My hand is stuffed with mode, design, device.
But I lack access to my proper stone.
And plenitude of plan shall not suffice
Nor grief nor love shall be enough alone
To ratify my little halves who bear
Across an autumn freezing everywhere.

The Womanhood

XV

Men of careful turns, haters of forks in the road,
The strain at the eye, that puzzlement, that awe —
Grant me that I am human, that I hurt,
That I can cry.

Not that I now ask alms, in shame gone hollow,
Nor cringe outside the loud and sumptuous gate.
Admit me to our mutual estate.

Open my rooms, let in the light and air.
Reserve my service at the human feast.
And let the joy continue. Do not hoard silence
For the moment when I enter, tardily,
To enjoy my height among you. And to love you
No more as a woman loves a drunken mate,
Restraining full caress and good My Dear,
Even pity for the heaviness and the need —
Fearing sudden fire out of the uncaring mouth,
Boiling in the slack eyes, and the traditional blow.
Next, the indifference formal, deep and slow.

Comes in your graceful glider and benign,
To smile upon me bigly; now desires
Me easy, easy; claims the days are softer
Than they were; murmurs reflectively "Remember
When cruelty, metal, public, uncomplex,
Trampled you obviously and every hour. . . ."
(Now cruelty flaunts diplomas, is elite,
Delicate, has polish, knows how to be discreet):
    Requests my patience, wills me to be calm,
    Brings me a chair, but the one with broken straw,
    Whispers "My friend, no thing is without flaw.
    If prejudice is native — and it is — you
    Will find it ineradicable — not to
    Be juggled, not to be altered at all,
    But left unvexed at its place in the properness
    Of things, even to be given (with grudging) honor.
        What
    We are to hope is that intelligence
    Can sugar up our prejudice with politeness.
    Politeness will take care of what needs caring.
    For the line is there.
    And has a meaning. So our fathers said —
    And they were wise — we think — At any rate,
    They were older than ourselves. And the report is
    What's old is wise. At any rate, the line is

Long and electric. Lean beyond and nod.
Be sprightly. Wave. Extend your hand and teeth.
But never forget it stretches there beneath."
The toys are all grotesque
And not for lovely hands; are dangerous,
Serrate in open and artful places. Rise.
Let us combine. There are no magics or elves
Or timely godmothers to guide us. We are lost, must
Wizard a track through our own screaming weed.

The Blackstone Rangers

I

AS SEEN BY DISCIPLINES

There they are.
Thirty at the corner.
Black, raw, ready.
Sores in the city
that do not want to heal.

II

THE LEADERS

Jeff. Gene. Geronimo. And Bop.
They cancel, cure and curry.
Hardly the dupes of the downtown thing
the cold bonbon,
the rhinestone thing. And hardly
in a hurry.
Hardly Belafonte, King,
Black Jesus, Stokely, Malcolm X or Rap.
Bungled trophies.
Their country is a Nation on no map.

Jeff, Gene, Geronimo and Bop
in the passionate noon,
in bewitching night

are the detailed men, the copious men.
They curry, cure,
they cancel, cancelled images whose Concerts
are not divine, vivacious; the different tins
are intense last entries; pagan argument;
translations of the night.

The Blackstone bitter bureaus
(bureaucracy is footloose) edit, fuse
unfashionable damnations and descent;
and exulting, monstrous hand on monstrous hand,
construct, strangely, a monstrous pearl or grace.

III

GANG GIRLS

A Rangerette

Gang Girls are sweet exotics.
Mary Ann
uses the nutrients of her orient,
but sometimes sighs for Cities of blue and jewel
beyond her Ranger rim of Cottage Grove.
(Bowery Boys, Disciples, Whip-Birds will
dissolve no margins, stop no savory sanctities.)

Mary is
a rose in a whiskey glass.

Mary's
Februaries shudder and are gone. Aprils
fret frankly, lilac hurries on.
Summer is a hard irregular ridge.
October looks away.
And that's the Year!
        Save for her bugle-love.
Save for the bleat of not-obese devotion.
Save for Somebody Terribly Dying, under
the philanthropy of robins. Save for her Ranger
bringing

an amount of rainbow in a string-drawn bag.
"Where did you get the diamond?" Do not ask:
but swallow, straight, the spirals of his flask
and assist him at your zipper; pet his lips
and help him clutch you.

Love's another departure.
Will there be any arrivals, confirmations?
Will there be gleaning?

Mary, the Shakedancer's child
from the rooming-flat, pants carefully, peers at
her laboring lover. . . .
            Mary! Mary Ann!
Settle for sandwiches! settle for stocking caps!
for sudden blood, aborted carnival,
the props and niceties of non-loneliness —
the rhymes of Leaning.

Malcolm X

For Dudley Randall

Original.
Ragged-round.
Rich-robust.

He had the hawk-man's eyes.
We gasped. We saw the maleness.
The maleness raking out and making guttural the air
and pushing us to walls.

And in a soft and fundamental hour
a sorcery devout and vertical
beguiled the world.

He opened us —
who was a key,

who was a man.

Dudley Randall (1914-   )

Dudley Randall, founder of the Broadside Press, has written poetry, fiction, and articles. Born in Washington, D. C., he received his Bachelor's degree from Wayne State University and a Master's in library science from the University of Michigan. Winner of the Tompkins Award for poetry, he has published two collections: *Poem Counterpoem* (1966), in collaboration with Margaret Danner, and *Cities Burning* (1968).

Primitives

Paintings with stiff
homuncules, flat in iron
draperies, with distorted
bodies against spaceless
landscapes.

Poems of old
poets in stiff
metres whose harsh
syllables
drag like
dogs with
crushed
backs.

We go back to
them, spurn difficult
grace and
symmetry,
paint tri-faced

107

monsters,
write lines that
do not sing, or
even croak, but that
bump,
jolt, and are hacked
off in the mid-
dle, as if by these dis-
tortions, this
magic, we can
exorcise
horror, which we
have seen and fear to
see again:

hate deified,
fears and
guilt conquering,
turning cities to
gas, powder and a
little rubble.

The Melting Pot

There is a magic melting pot
where any girl or man
can step in Czech or Greek or Scot,
step out American.

Johann and **Jan** and **Jean** and **Juan,**
Giovanni and **Ivan**
step in and then step out again
all freshly christened **John.**

Sam, watching, said, "Why, I was here
even before they came,"
and stepped in too, but was tossed out
before he passed the brim.

And every time Sam tried that pot
they threw him out again.
"Keep out. This is our private pot.
We don't want your black stain."

At last, thrown out a thousand times,
Sam said, "I don't give a damn.
Shove your old pot. You can like it or not,
but I'll be just what I am."

Naomi Long Madgett (1923-   )

Born in Norfolk, Virginia, reared in New Jersey and Missouri, Naomi Long Madgett received a Bachelor's from Virginia State College and a Master's from Wayne State University. A teacher of English in high school and college, recipient of fellowships for writing and once honored as "English Teacher of the Year" in Detroit, she has published three volumes of poetry: *Songs to a Phantom Nightingale, One and the Many,* and *Star by Star.*

Nocturne

See how dark the night settles on my face,
How deep the rivers of my soul
Flow imperturbable and strong.

Rhythms of unremembered jungles
Pulse through the untamed shadows of my song,
And my cry is the dusky accent of secret midnight birds.

Above the sable valleys of my sorrow
My swarthy hands have fashioned
Pyramids of virgin joy.

See how tenderly God pulls His blanket of blackness over the earth.
You think I am not beautiful?
You lie!

Alabama Centennial

They said, "Wait." Well, I waited.
For a hundred years I waited

111

In cotton fields, kitchens, balconies,
In bread lines, at back doors, on chain gangs,
In stinking "colored" toilets
And crowded ghettos,
Outside of schools and voting booths.
And some said, "Later."
And some said, "Never!"

Then a new wind blew, and a new voice
Rode its wings with quiet urgency,
Strong, determined, sure.
"No," it said. "Not 'never,' not 'later,'
Not even 'soon.'
Now.
Walk!"

And other voices echoed the freedom words,
"Walk together, children don't get weary,"
Whispered them, sang them, prayed them, shouted them.
"Walk!"
And I walked the streets of Montgomery
Until a link in the chain of patient acquiescence broke.

Then again: Sit down!
And I sat down at the counters of Greensboro.
Ride! And I rode the bus for freedom.
Kneel! And I went down on my knees in prayer and faith.
March! And I'll march until the last chain falls
Singing, "We shall overcome."

Not all the dogs and hoses in Birmingham
Nor all the clubs and guns in Selma
Can turn this tide.
Not all the jails can hold these young black faces
From their destiny of manhood,
Of equality, of dignity,
Of the American Dream
A hundred years past due.
Now!

Darwin T. Turner (1931-   )

The grandson of Dr. Charles Henry Turner, an eminent biologist, Darwin T. Turner, born and reared in Cincinnati, Ohio, graduated, Phi Beta Kappa, from the University of Cincinnati in 1947 with a B.A. in English. He earned an M.A. (English, 1949) from the same institution and a Ph.D. (English, 1956) from the University of Chicago. He has taught English at Clark College and Morgan State College; has chaired English departments at Florida A. and M. University and North Carolina A. and T. State University; and has served as visiting professor at the University of Wisconsin. Presently he is Dean of the Graduate School of North Carolina A. and T. State University.

In addition to serving as president or a member of governing boards of several professional societies, Darwin Turner has published critical studies on drama, Afro-American literature, American literature, and literary criticism in various journals. He has co-edited *Images of the Negro in America* and is the author of *Nathaniel Hawthorne's The Scarlet Letter.* He has also written short stories, drama, and poetry. *Katharsis* is his only published volume of poetry.

The Sit-in

Patient, we pray and wait and weep and pray.
Our faces are ridged; our faces are black —
Black mirrors of a cancerous, imbedded rack
Of festered hate stretching our souls today.
Our stomachs knot in ulcered, entrailed clay;
Our eyes flame pain of sleepless, voiceless fears;
Our song has choked on spittle of shame and tears.

113

But patient we weep, and patient we pray:
"Teach us, God, in this moment's hate and pain
To taste the Judas kiss and cry, 'Forgive,'
To wear the centuries' crown of thorns and live
In grace to know our wait was not in vain."

But louder surges thought incessantly,
"He died for us. For what in hell do we?"

Death

Death is not a dream; death lives:
the shadow at the corner of the eye,
the steps that trail along a dawn-damp street,
the window's sudden face.

The young — warm-blanketed, head poked out —
the young can damn Death:
a playmate
carelessly cast into dim and distant corners
with geese of golden eggs
and giants of steps of seven leagues
and magic swords and witches' candy houses
that fret and fright and swirl into
a tucking-in, feet-warm, goodnight kiss.

Youth can yearn Death:
laurel seized to shake in spite
at the forehead-furrowed alive and left behind;
Elysian fields of peace for the alone,
the not-understood,
the first feet in new snow along the worn path.

Age knows Death.
One day a friend, an offered cigarette,
a laugh and idle compliment,
a breathing-in and breathing-out of life;
the next, a hushed report,
a solemn shaking of the head,
a line or two of type —
another gone before the shock has time to thaw.

And then we pray
and think
and fear
and backward crawl
into the magnet of indifferent Night.

Love

I have known what it is to love:
to walk among the midday mob,
and share the friendship of the faceless throng;
to laugh with children on the paths,
and chatter at a bright-eyed squirrel.
I have known what it is to love:
afraid to speak,
fearing it would be thought a lie;
afraid to breathe a smoke-ring dream
and watch it fade,
or see it ground beneath a careless toe.
I have known what it is to love
and hear a sigh —
soft as worn string that parts —
and not to know it as my own.
I have known what it is to love:
to walk the tower-shadowed streets
and seek one face;
to shudder at cacophony of horns and brakes,
and listen for one voice.
I have known what it is to love:
to seek to hide the thought
in Lethal wine and laughing eyes
and kisses from a dozen pairs
of painted lips.
I have known what it is to love,
and tongue the alum of
a lonely heart.

Sonnet Sequence

I

You are but these to me: a freckled face,
Soft-lighted by a fragile smile, from lips

And eyes that shade a sorrow's ghost; a grace
As lightly balanced as a lark that dips
In restless pause before he seeks the stars;
A childyoung voice, that lullabies me peace,
Secure and warm, from life's diurnal wars
That fret the lonely mind without surcease.
You are remembered scent, imprinted on
A chair; a careless touch that burns within;
A glance that kisses from a table's length;
A subtle difference that you bring into
A room. But most, you are the woman
Who has taught me what it is to love.

FINALE

How carelessly the poet sings love's pains.
Sure-cushioned in a flint-cased mind, he sighs
The tears that trickle from the loveblind eyes;
The purifying grief that purging, drains
The sin-sick soul, and cleanses it of stains,
As rain gentles soot from wan winter's dawn;
The "glad-girl" heart that smiles, when storms have gone,
"It's better to have loved," the ancient strains.
Much grimmer is the weary gardener's fate,
When first he finds the heart, in wayward yield,
Has trampled flowers nursed through patient years:
No time to chide the mind, nor time for tears;
Time but to mend the wall, re-seed the field,
And hire a sterner will to guard the gate.

Guest Lecturer

The evening, ending.
          Already only memory:
The lights upon his face and hair;
The human shapes which nodded, laughed,
          And breathed on tonal cue;
Applause that chattered for a second bow;
Crowding, clutching compliments;
The thrust of challenge;

The tongues and hands and eyes
   Of Adoration presumed.
      Now:
A caterer crumbs the folded cloth
   And drains the silver urn
While he,
   Clinging to a question,
Evades the fretting host,
   Charon to the dreaded end:
A needed, not wanted, lingered
   Bourbon;
The room —
Which has no stage.

LeRoi Jones (1934-   )

LeRoi Jones has become a spokesman and a leader for many young black people who are rebelling against traditions of society and art. Born in Newark, New Jersey, he attended the Newark branch of Rutgers University before transferring to Howard University to complete his undergraduate education. After serving in the Army Air Force, Jones returned to civilian life as a teacher and a writer. He founded the Black Arts Repertory Theatre in Harlem and has directed Spirit House in Newark.

The recipient of a Guggenheim fellowship, Jones first attracted attention with *Preface to a Twenty-Volume Suicide Note* (1961), a volume of poems characterized by vigorous language and powerful imagery. His subsequent work has been influential and controversial. The techniques of *The System of Dante's Hell*, a novel, are studied by many young writers. His interpretation of the history of black people through their experience — *Blues People* — is a persuasive one. His plays have created sensation because of their revolutionary thought, violent language, and fervent denunciations of white racism. *Dutchman*, the best-known, was judged the best off-Broadway production of 1963-64. *The Slave, The Baptism,* and *The Toilet* are other well-known plays. His most recent collection — *Tales* (1967) — mingles sketches, essays, and stories in what some writers believe to be a laudable effort to achieve greater flexibility for the short-story form. In 1968, he co-edited *Black Fire*, an anthology of black revolutionary literature.

Since 1964, Jones has concentrated on the use of literature — poetry and drama especially — as the force of revolution. To this end, he has revised his poetic style to make it more meaningful for community residents who have found little relevance in the traditional, formal language of American poetry. His success is evidenced in the extreme popularity of his frequent public readings in community assemblies. Thus, Jones has revitalized poetry for many people.

119

The following selections, however, are from Jones' second book and mark a stage at which, still using traditional style and language, he was exploring his own psyche.

An Agony. As Now.

I am inside someone
who hates me. I look
out from his eyes. Smell
what fouled tunes come in
to his breath. Love his
wretched women.

Slits in the metal, for sun. Where
my eyes sit turning, at the cool air
the glance of light, or hard flesh
rubbed against me, a woman, a man,
without shadow, or voice, or meaning.

This is the enclosure (flesh,
where innocence is a weapon. An
abstraction. Touch. (Not mine.
Or yours, if you are the soul I had
and abandoned when I was blind and had
my enemies carry me as a dead man
(if he is beautiful, or pitied.

It can be pain. (As now, as all his
flesh hurts me.) It can be that. Or
pain. As when she ran from me into
that forest.
        Or pain, the mind
silver spiraled whirled against the
sun, higher than even old men thought
God would be. Or pain. And the other. The
yes. (Inside his books, his fingers. They
are withered yellow flowers and were never
beautiful.) The yes. You will, lost soul, say
'beauty.' Beauty, practiced, as the tree. The
slow river. A white sun in its wet sentences.

The end of man is his beauty

And silence
which proves / but
a referent
to my disorder.
                    Your world shakes

cities die
beneath your shape.

   The single shadow

at noon
like a live tree
whose leaves
are like clouds
Weightless soul
at whose love faith moves
as a dark and
withered day.

They speak of singing who
have never heard song; of living
whose deaths are legends
for their kind.

            A scream
gathered in wet fingers,
at the top of its stalk.

— They have passed
and gone
whom you thot your lovers

In this perfect quiet, my friend,
their shapes
are not unlike
night's

Etheridge Knight (1933-   )

In her introduction to Etheridge Knight's *Poems from Prison*, Gwendolyn Brooks called attention to their masculinity, centers of softness, warmth, music, and blackness — "freed and terrible and beautiful." Born in Corinth, Mississippi, a veteran of the United States Army, Knight was sentenced to Indiana State Prison in 1960. His poems and stories written there have established his reputation as one of the promising new black writers.

The Idea of Ancestry

1

Taped to the wall of my cell are 47 pictures: 47 black
faces: my father, mother, grandmothers (1 dead), grand
fathers (both dead), brothers, sisters, uncles, aunts,
cousins (1st & 2nd), nieces, and nephews. They stare
across the space at me sprawling on my bunk. I know
their dark eyes, they know mine. I know their style,
they know mine. I am all of them, they are all of me;
they are farmers, I am a thief, I am me, they are thee.

I have at one time or another been in love with my mother,
1 grandmother, 2 sisters, 2 aunts (1 went to the asylum),
and 5 cousins. I am now in love with a 7 yr old niece
(she sends me letters written in large block print, and
her picture is the only one that smiles at me).

I have the same name as 1 grandfather, 3 cousins, 3 nephews,
and 1 uncle. The uncle disappeared when he was 15, just took
off and caught a freight (they say). He's discussed each year
when the family has a reunion, he causes uneasiness in

123

the clan, he is an empty space. My father's mother, who is 93
and who keeps the Family Bible with everybody's birth dates
(and death dates) in it, always mentions him. There is no
place in her Bible for "whereabouts unknown."

He Sees Through Stone

He sees through stone
he has the secret
eyes this old black one
who under prison skies
sits pressed by the sun
against the western wall
his pipe between purple gums

the years fall
like overripe plums
bursting red flesh
on the dark earth

his time is not my time
but I have known him
in a time gone

he led me trembling cold
into the dark forest
taught me the secret rites
to take a woman
to be true to my brothers
to make my spear drink
the blood
of my enemies

now black cats circle him
flash white teeth
snarl at the air
mashing green grass beneath
shining muscles
ears peeling his words
he smiles
he knows
the hunt   the enemy
he has the secret eyes
he sees through stone

Don L. Lee (1942-   )

Born in 1942, Don Lee, author of three slim volumes of poetry and a broadside, is particularly well-known in Chicago, where he has taught at Roosevelt University, and throughout Illinois, Michigan, and Wisconsin, where audiences have been excited by his poems and his dramatic readings of them. Although he has written lyrics on traditional themes, most of his poetry exemplifies the revolutionary creed of the Black Arts Movement, with emphasis on black language, nontraditional structure, and thought which is immediately relevant to black people. His latest collection is *Don't Cry! Scream!* (1969). The following selections are from his second book, *Think Black* (1968).

Education

I had a good teacher,
He taught me everything I know;
how to lie,
     cheat,
     and how to strike the softest blow.

My teacher thought himself to be wise and right
He taught me things most people consider nice;
  such as to pray,
      smile,
      and how not to fight.

My teacher taught me other things too,
Things that I will be forever looking at;
  how to berate.
     segregate,
     and how to be inferior without hate.

My teacher's wisdom forever grows,
He taught me things every child will know;
   how to steal,
      appeal,
         and accept most things against my will.

All these acts take as facts,
The mistake was made in teaching me
How not to be BLACK.

Back Again, Home
(confessions of an ex-executive)

Pains of insecurity surround me;
   shined shoes,
   conservative suits,
   button down shirts with silk ties.
   bi-weekly payroll.

Ostracized, but not knowing why;
   executive haircut,
   clean shaved,
   "yes" instead of "yeah" and "no" instead of "naw",
   hours, nine to five. (after five he's alone)

"Doing an excellent job, keep it up;"
   promotion made — semi-monthly payroll,
   very quiet — never talks,
   budget balanced — saved the company money,
   quality work — production tops.
   He looks sick. (but there is a smile in his eyes)

He resigned, we wonder why;
   let his hair grow — a mustache too,
   out of a job — broke and hungry,
   friends are coming back — bring food,
   not quiet now — trying to speak,
   what did he say?

   "Back Again,

      BLACK AGAIN,

         Home."

A. Selected Collections by Individual Authors

Bontemps, Arna. *Personals*. London: Breman, 1963.

Braithwaite, William Stanley. *The House of Falling Leaves*. Boston: Luce, 1908.

Braithwaite, William Stanley. *Lyrics of Life and Love*. Boston: Turner, 1904.

Braithwaite, William Stanley. *Selected Poems*. New York: Coward-McCann, 1948.

Brooks, Gwendolyn. *Annie Allen*. New York: Harper and Bros., 1949.

Brooks, Gwendolyn. *The Bean Eaters*. New York, Harper and Bros., 1960.

Brooks, Gwendolyn. *Bronzeville Boys and Girls*. New York: Harper and Bros., 1956.

Brooks, Gwendolyn. *In the Mecca*. New York: Harper and Bros., 1968.

Brooks, Gwendolyn. *Selected Poems*. New York: Harper and Bros., 1963.

Brooks, Gwendolyn. *A Street in Bronzeville*. New York: Harper and Bros., 1945.

Brown, Sterling A. *Southern Road*. New York: Harcourt, Brace, 1932.

Cotter, Joseph Seamon, Jr. *The Band of Gideon and Other Lyrics*. Boston: Cornhill, 1918.

Cotter, Joseph Seamon, Sr. *Collected Poems of Joseph S. Cotter Sr.* New York: Harrison, 1938.

Cotter, Joseph Seamon, Sr. *Sequel to the "Pied Piper of Hamelin," and Other Poems*. New York: Harrison, 1939.

Cotter, Joseph Seamon, Sr. *A White Song and a Black One*. Louisville, Ky.: Bradley and Gilbert, 1909.

Cullen, Countee. *The Ballad of the Brown Girl; an Old Ballad Retold*. New York: Harper, 1927.

Cullen, Countee. *The Black Christ and Other Poems*. New York: Harper, 1929.

Cullen, Countee. *Color*. New York: Harper, 1925.

Cullen, Countee. *Copper Sun*. New York: Harper, 1927.

Cullen, Countee. *The Lost Zoo; by Countee Cullen and Christopher Cat*. New York: Harper, 1940. [For children.]

Cullen, Countee. *The Medea and Some Poems*. New York: Harper, 1935.

Cullen, Countee. *On These I Stand*. New York: Harper, 1947.

Cuney, Waring. *Puzzles*. Selected and introduced by Paul Breman. Utrecht, Holland: Breman, 1961.

Davis, Frank Marshall. *Black Man's Verse*. Chicago: Black Cat, 1935.

Davis, Frank Marshall. *47th Street Poems*. Prairie City, Ill.: Decker, 1948.

Dodson, Owen. *Powerful Long Ladder*. New York: Farrar, Straus, 1946.

Dunbar, Paul Laurence. *The Complete Poems of Paul Laurence Dunbar*. New York: Dodd, Mead, 1913.

Dunbar, Paul Laurence. *Lyrics of the Hearthside*. New York: Dodd, Mead, 1899.

Dunbar, Paul Laurence. *Lyrics of Love and Laughter*. New York: Dodd, Mead, 1903.

Dunbar, Paul Laurence. *Lyrics of Lowly Life*. New York: Dodd, Mead, 1896.

Dunbar, Paul Laurence. *Lyrics of Sunshine and Shadow*. New York: Dodd, Mead, 1905.

Dunbar, Paul Laurence. *Majors and Minors*. Toledo, Ohio: Hadley and Hadley, 1895. [Actually pub. 1896]

Dunbar, Paul Laurence. *Oak and Ivy*. Dayton, Ohio: United Brethren, 1893 [Actually pub. 1892]

Emanuel, James A. *The Treehouse and Other Poems*. Detroit: Broadside, 1968.

Harper, Frances Ellen Watkins. *Poems*. Philadelphia: Ferguson, 1895.

Harper, Frances Ellen Watkins. *Poems on Miscellaneous Subjects*. Philadelphia: Merrihew, 1874.

Hayden, Robert E. *A Ballad of Remembrance*. London: Breman, 1962.

Hayden, Robert E. *Figure of Time*. Nashville: Hemphill, 1955.

Hayden, Robert E. *Heart-Shape in the Dust*. Detroit: Falcon, 1940.

Hayden, Robert E. *The Lion and the Archer*. New York: Hemphill, 1949.

Hayden, Robert E. *Selected Poems*. New York: October House, 1966.

Hill, Roy L. *49 Poems*. Manhattan, Kansas: Agsic Press, 1968.

Hill, Leslie Pinckney. *Wings of Oppression and Other Poems.* Boston: Stratford, 1921.

Hughes, Langston. *Ask Your Mama: 12 Moods for Jazz.* New York: Knopf, 1961.

Hughes, Langston. *The Dream Keeper and Other Poems.* New York: Knopf, 1932.

Hughes, Langston. *Fields of Wonder.* New York: Knopf, 1947.

Hughes, Langston. *Fine Clothes to the Jew.* New York: Knopf, 1927.

Hughes, Langston. *Montage of a Dream Deferred.* New York: Holt, 1951.

Hughes, Langston. *One-Way Ticket.* New York: Knopf, 1949.

Hughes, Langston. *The Panther and the Lash: Poems of Our Times.* New York: Knopf, 1967.

Hughes, Langston. *Scottsboro Limited: Four Poems and A Play in Verse.* New York: Golden Stair, 1932.

Hughes, Langston. *The Selected Poems of Langston Hughes.* New York: Knopf, 1965.

Hughes, Langston. *Shakespeare in Harlem.* New York: Knopf, 1942.

Hughes, Langston. *The Weary Blues.* New York: Knopf, 1926.

Johnson, Fenton. *A Little Dreaming.* Chicago: Peterson, 1913.

Johnson, Fenton. *Vision of the Dusk.* New York: [the author] 1915.

Johnson, Georgia Douglas. *An Autumn Love Cycle.* New York: Neal, 1938.

Johnson, Georgia Douglas. *Bronze: A Book of Verse.* Boston: Brimmer, 1922.

Johnson, Georgia Douglas. *The Heart of a Woman and Other Poems.* Boston: Cornhill, 1918.

Johnson, James Weldon. *Fifty Years and Other Poems.* Boston: Cornhill, 1917.

Johnson, James Weldon. *God's Trombones; Seven Negro Sermons in Verse.* New York: Viking, 1927.

Johnson, James Weldon. *Saint Peter Relates an Incident; Selected Poems.* New York: Viking, 1935.

Jones, LeRoi. *The Dead Lecturer.* New York: Grove, 1964.

Jones, LeRoi. *Preface to a Twenty-Volume Suicide Note.* New York: Corinth, 1961.

Knight, Etheridge. *Poems from Prison.* Detroit: Broadside, 1968.

Lee, Don. *Black Pride.* Detroit: Broadside, 1968.

Lee, Don. *Don't Cry! Scream!* Detroit: Broadside, 1969.

Lee, Don. *Think Black*. Detroit: Broadside, 1968.

Lorde, Audre. *The First Cities*. New York: Poets, 1967.

McGirt, James E. *Avenging the Maine*. Raleigh, N.C.: Edward & Broughton, 1899.

McKay, Claude. *Harlem Shadows*. New York: Harcourt, Brace, 1922.

McKay, Claude. *Selected Poems*. New York: Bookman, 1953.

McKay, Claude. *Spring in New Hampshire and Other Poems*. London: Richards, 1920.

Madgett, Naomi Long. *One and the Many*. New York: Exposition, 1956

Madgett, Naomi Long. *Songs to a Phantom Nightingale*. New York: Fortuny's, 1941.

Madgett, Naomi Long. *Star by Star*. Detroit, Mich.: Harlo, 1965.

Randall, Dudley. *Cities Burning*. Detroit: Broadside, 1968.

Rivers, Conrad Kent. *The Black Bodies and This Sunburnt Face*. Cleveland: Free Lance, 1963.

Spellman, A. B. *The Beautiful Days*. New York: Poet's Press, 1965.

Tolson, Melvin B. *Harlem Gallery, Book I: The Curator*. New York: Twayne, 1965.

Tolson, Melvin B. *Libretto for the Republic of Liberia*. New York: Twayne, 1953.

Tolson, Melvin B. *Rendezvous with America*. New York: Dodd, Mead, 1944.

Turner, Darwin T. *Katharsis*. Wellesley, Mass.: Wellesley P., 1964.

Walker, Margaret. *For My People*. New Haven, Conn.: Yale U P, 1942.

Whitman, Albery Allson. *An Idyl of the South: An Epic Poem in Two Parts*. Metaphysical, 1901.

Whitman, Albery Allson. *Not a Man, and Yet a Man*. Springfield, Ohio: Republic, 1877.

Whitman, Albery Allson. *The Rape of Florida*. 3rd ed. St. Louis: Nixon-Jones, 1890.

B. Selected Anthologies Including Poems

Brown, Sterling A., Arthur P. Davis, and Ulysses Lee, eds. *The Negro Caravan*. New York: Dryden, 1941.

Calverton, Victor F., ed. *An Anthology of American Negro Literature*. New York: Random, 1929.

Chapman, Abraham, ed. *Black Voices*. New York: Dell, 1968.

Emanuel, James A., and Gross, Theodore L. *Dark Symphony: Negro Literature in America*. New York: The Free Press, 1968.

Hughes, Langston, and Arna Bontemps, eds. *The Poetry of the Negro, 1746-1949*. Garden City, N.Y.: Doubleday, 1949.

Johnson, Charles S., ed. *Ebony and Topaz: A Collectanea*. New York: National Urban League, 1927.

Johnson, James W., ed. *The Book of American Negro Poetry*. Rev. ed. New York: Harcourt, Brace, 1931.

Jones, LeRoi, and Larry Neal, eds. *Black Fire*. New York: Morrow, 1968.

Kerlin, Robert T., ed. *Contemporary Poetry of the Negro*. Hampton, Va.: Hampton Institute P, 1923.

Kerlin, Robert T., ed. *Negro Poets and Their Poems*. 2nd ed. Washington: Associated Pub., 1935.

Lanussee, Armand, ed. *Creole Voices: Poems in French by Free Men of Color*. Centennial ed. Washington: Associated Pub., 1945.

Locke, Alain, ed. *Four Negro Poets*. New York: Simon and Schuster, 1927.

Major, Clarence, ed. *The New Black Poetry*. New York: International Pub., 1969.

Marcus, Samuel, ed. *Anthology of Revolutionary Poetry*. New York: Active, 1929.

Murphy, Beatrice, ed. *Ebony Rhythm*. New York: Exposition, 1948.

Murphy, Beatrice, ed. *Negro Voices; An Anthology of Contemporary Verse*. New York: Harrison, 1938.

Perez Echavarria, Miguel Ramon, ed. *La poesia negra en America.* Buenos Aires: Nocito & Rano, 1946.

Perkins, Eugene, ed. *Black Expressions: An Anthology of New Black Poets.* Chicago: Conda, 1967.

Pool, Rosey E., ed. *Beyond the Blues: New Poems by American Negroes.* Lympne, Kent, England: Hand and Flower, 1962.

Pool, Rosey E., ed. *Black and Unknown Bards.* Aldington, Kent, England: Hand and Flower, 1958.

Schulmann, R. Baird, ed. *Nine Black Poets.* Durham, N. C.: Moore, 1968.

Ten: Anthology of Detroit Poets. Fort Smith, Ark.: South and West, 1968.

Watkins, Sylvester C., ed. *Anthology of American Negro Literature.* New York: Random, 1944.

White, Newman and W. C. Jackson, eds. *An Anthology of Verse by American Negroes.* Durham, N. C.: Moore, 1968.